MUSTERING THE STRENGTH TO FIGHT

Tasha Odunuyi

Mustering the Strength to Fight © 2020
by Tasha Odunuyi. All Rights Reserved.

All rights reserved. No part of this book may be reproduced in any form or by any electronic or mechanical means including information storage and retrieval systems, without permission in writing from the author. The only exception is by a reviewer, who may quote short excerpts in a review.

The Holy Bible, New International Version®, NIV® Copyright © 1973, 1978, 1984, 2011 by Biblica, Inc.® Used by permission. All rights reserved worldwide.

Cover designed by Octavius Holmes

Printed in the United States of America
First Printing: December 2020
The Scribe Tribe Publishing Group

THE SCRIBE TRIBE
PUBLISHING GROUP

ISBN-978-1-7352568-6-3 (print)
ISBN-978-1-735268-7-0 (electronic)

*To three pieces that are missing
from the world,
but never from my heart.
Also, to the grieved, the pained
and the traumatized.*

ROUND ONE

Welcome to the Fight!

There are no pleasures in a fight, but some of my fights have been a pleasure to win.
—Muhammad Ali

I had recently birthed my last child and opened a salon in a room off my garage so that I could be home with my children. It was just like a normal busy Friday in the salon. Clients were booked through the end of the day, but I can remember feeling off. I was a bit anxious and carried some type of anxiety throughout the whole day. I couldn't quite figure it out, but my spirit was uneasy with so much unrest.

I was extremely tired but had promised my older two children that we would go to the mall after work. Exhausted and feeling frustrated, I bundled up my 3-month-old baby along with my 5 and 8-year-olds, and we were off. It was very strange, but for some reason my children were not their usual selves. I'd never had issues with them in the store because they knew better. However, the baby was crying more than usual and my older two were whiny. It was one heck of a trip. Honestly, I don't remember even making it to the register.

Once I finally got the kids home, I fed and put them to bed then took a few minutes to sit in my salon before getting up to shampoo my hair. All I wanted to do was relax after a long trying day with work and children. The highlight was going to be sitting under the dryer to unwind from the day.

I sat there falling asleep constantly bumping my head against the dryer when the phone rang permanently awaking me from my nap. At that point I was all talked out and ignored the call until it kept ringing back to back. When I finally answered my heart sank to the ground and I almost passed out from the rush that went to my heart. I was speechless and couldn't move. What I heard on the other line stopped me in my tracks. I tried so hard not to scream, but I was in a panic. Have you ever had that feeling of wanting to say something but couldn't get it out? Wanting to move but feeling like you're frozen in time? I stood there trying to process that one of my brothers had just been stabbed during a family altercation with two of my other brothers. My heart just sank.

My mom called from the hospital and said we should hurry up and get there. She gave no details other than that my brother was just rushed there with a stab wound, but I could hear the fear in her voice. For several minutes, my heart raced in a panic trying to process what I heard on the other line. Not knowing what to do or how to even think logically through what I should do next left me paralyzed. The anxiety, panic and confusion arose over my body and I was disoriented until I did my best to calm myself down.

My husband was on a business trip and not due to drive back until later that night. After several unsuccessful attempts to reach him, I just left a message. Once I finally processed as best as I could under the circumstances, I phoned my neighbor and asked if she could come and stay with my children while I headed to the hospital. By the time my neighbor arrived, my sister and I rushed to get in the car to safely make our way to Christ Hospital. My hair was still wet, I had on my salon jacket, and rollers were falling out of my head! I was just a total mess, but relieved that we were on our way.

    I kept praying and crying out to God to help get my sister and I safely to the hospital. I could barely think straight, much less be in the right frame of mind to drive. We were distraught and crying the whole way. My heart was beating so fast that I was visibly shaking and having palpitations. I was terrified because I didn't think I could drive us safely but had no other choice because at the time my sister didn't know how to drive.

    My brother had spent the weekend with me, and I just dropped him off the day before. Just reflecting on all of that caused me to be overwhelmed with emotion. *What is happening? Is this real? Someone please tell me I am having a bad dream!* That was all I could think.

    As we cried and I drove, it dawned on me that my husband's friend lived along the route to the hospital so I stopped there with hopes that he or his wife would be able to drive us. We pulled up to his house, rang the doorbell, and banged on the door desperately weak and in a panic. There was a car parked in the driveway, but no one answered so I hopped back in my car and asked God to please guide me and get us there safely. There was no other way.

    I whizzed through traffic, crying, and screaming, wishing every car would just get out of my way. I practically ran every light and it still seemed like we would never get there. It's just by the grace of God that I wasn't pulled over for erratic driving. But at the time I didn't care. I just wanted to see my brother and understand what happened.

As I drove, my sister got a call from my neighbor who was with the kids and my life practically flashed before my eyes. She informed us that my brother had died before we could make it to the hospital. I screamed asking how she knew and who told her that. My mom called my neighbor looking for me and she called my sister.

We were still driving trying to make our way. *Why is everyone driving so slowly?* It felt like time stopped when I heard that he had passed away. The further we drove, the further it seemed like we had to drive. My guardian angels had to have been with us because there was no way I could have safely arrived without the help of God.

When we finally arrived, we ran inside to the front desk hysterically crying. The receptionist directed us to the floor he was on. Once we stepped foot off the elevator all I saw was my mom there alone crying uncontrollably. She had no family or friends to comfort her. Only the chaplain was there trying to console her.

We totally lost it. *How could this be? What? A fight? Stabbed? Altercation with my other brothers?* My mind just couldn't process all that was happening. All I could do was fall onto my knees in the hospital. I was hitting the wall and screaming 'why' when I felt someone grab me. I turned around to see that my husband had made it to the hospital.

By then other family members started arriving. It was chaotic. Everyone was dazed with the look of sadness on each face. We were struggling to come to grips with my brother's death. The hospital staff directed us to his room. His body was still warm just like he was resting. *What am I looking at?* A lifeless body. I couldn't wrap my head around the how and why. *Why and how on earth could this be? My brother dying under these tragic circumstances? He was just with me.*

While I spent those last moments at my brother's side, the doctors rushed in to ask if he was an organ donor. *Damn, he just died and you want to take his organs? Leave me alone!* Delirious and angry at the thought, my body language spoke for me causing the doctor to walk off and leave me alone.

I was in such a bad way that they had to take me outside on the rooftop of Christ Hospital just so I could get some fresh air and calm down. I was pacing back and forth, hyperventilating, and screaming, "Jesus help me." I just didn't know what else to do. Never in a million years did I think that was why I had a bad feeling all day. Never did I think I could ever get a call like that about someone in my own family. I've always heard about things like this but never imagined it happening to me.

There came the moment when my family started asking about my brother being a donor because the doctor was pressuring them for an answer. Honestly, I can't remember how it happened, but I know eventually I angrily screamed 'yes!' I just wanted him to stop asking me about taking my brother's organs at a time like that. My brain could not even process that time was of the essence for them saving another life. But I wasn't thinking about another life. I was thinking of Lorenzo.

I was thinking about the fact that I was at a hospital and just saw my brother lying there lifeless. I was pondering the reality that one of my other brothers accidently killed him in a fight amongst themselves that got out of hand. I was wondering what state my brother was in and how the police were treating him. I was thinking about my third brother and worried about how he was holding up. He wasn't at the hospital either because both brothers were taken to the police station for questioning.

We eventually left the hospital and went home but it honestly felt like I needed someone to wake me up from a horrible nightmare. One brother lying dead at the hospital, one arrested for the act and the other one released from the police station totally distraught, sitting on my couch staring into space. It was so very overwhelming. *This can't be life right now.*

Between having my mom, brother, husband, and children to tend to I was a complete mess, but I couldn't stop worrying about my brother who was arrested and my other siblings. I couldn't imagine what those involved must have been going through. Since I only had limited information, I found myself trying to replay what I imagined happened in my mind. Clearly, it was impossible to digest. The only thing I knew for sure was that one was arrested. I didn't know any details about the fight and didn't think I could even handle knowing. I mean, anyone who has siblings has had a fight before; that's not uncommon. *But this?* That heated disagreement ended with death. It was surreal.

The next day, I asked my husband to drive me to the jail. I needed to see my brother. My husband was shocked and wanted to know if I was sure. He asked if I thought it was too soon. Family members acted surprised and bothered about me going, but I had already lost one brother and didn't want to lose another. And as long as I could help it, I wasn't going to. Everyone needs someone in their corner, and I knew in my heart that he would not have wanted to purposely kill our brother. He wasn't a murderer. As tragic as it was, God gave me the boldness and courage to muster up the strength needed to do what I know only He could have laid on my heart.

It could only be God. Less than 24 hours prior, I saw the news about our brother. God displayed unconditional love within me while hurting, confused and distraught at the mere thought that we were in that type of situation. There was no time for me to even think about how other people would take this. It wasn't about being selfish or insensitive and I didn't find fault in anyone who thought that maybe I was acting too fast. It was tragic.

That was family and I could not stand idly by and watch what looked like a movie play out. It wasn't a movie. It was real life and moving forward it would probably put me in so many situations that I could never have dreamed or prepared for. If God was all I had going forward, then I had all I needed. Only He would be able to sustain me and order my steps on how to move through something that had come and torn our family up leaving pure devastation. Havoc wreaked on our entire emotional state. We struggled mentally, physically, spiritually, and emotionally.

My husband agreed to take me. I was so anxious and nervous to see him. When I finally laid eyes on him, it took all the wind out of me seeing him dressed in all beige behind a glass wall. Unable to hug him or listen to his side of the story, tears streamed down my face. I couldn't bring myself to get the words out I wanted to say, and I think it made him feel like seeing him there bothered me. I am sure he wondered if I was forced to come against my will. Perhaps, the way I looked at him made him believe that I hated him or was immensely angry with him. At one point, with a melancholy look and his head hanging down, he asked my husband why he brought me there. My husband explained to him that no one forced me to come see him. That I needed to come and check on him. "She wanted to come," he replied. *Yep, I needed to see you.*

As I stood there totally hurt and confused with so many other emotions, all I could say was, "I love you and I'm here for you." He needed to know that no matter how ashamed, scared, confused and hurt he felt, he was not in it by himself. He was going to need some type of lifeline to help him manage getting through everything. It was something he would have to live with for the rest of his life. Every single day, sitting in jail locked up, he would be identified as a felon with a murder record. A number. No one would know or understand the details surrounding what took place. He would remember this every holiday, every birthday, every anniversary, every day.

Those were all the thoughts that went through my mind and allowed me to try as hard as I could to process the other side as we were all going through a family trauma. In retrospect, I realize God supernaturally empowered me with the strength to be there for my brother.

There was no way I could stand on the sidelines and let my brother go through that alone. It was tragic and he would need somebody. I pretty much tried as much as possible to put my feelings aside and go into fight mode. He was worth saving. Any life, regardless of the circumstances, is worth saving and God is the final judge. At the time, there definitely had to have been a divine encounter that came over me because the moves I made flowed so freely and without much thought. There was zero time to be mad or angry. I told my husband that I couldn't be angry at my brother and leave him alone in this. I just could not do it; I wasn't wired that way.

Having that act of compassion was something only God could give especially so soon after it happened. It didn't mean that he was my favorite brother or that I loved my now deceased sibling any less. I just knew that he was not a killer. Everything was surreal; it felt as if we were dealing with something out of a movie or news report. I could not believe that it was happening in real life. Many probably didn't understand my stance and it may have rubbed some the wrong way, but I had to step in. It didn't matter if I had to go at it alone, it needed to be done.

With my family still at my house, I begin to make funeral arrangements for my 20-year-old brother the following week. The house was in a complete uproar and business was on hold. It was my first time ever in that type of situation and I needed to make sure my brother was laid to rest in the best manner possible. The thought of making the funeral arrangements frightened me and gave so much anxiety but I had to make sure everything was in order for him. It was the least I could do. *But how am I going to get through this whole thing?*

There were so many things in front of me that needed a level of mental and physical strength I wasn't sure I had. The grief was overwhelming to a point that I couldn't explain even if I tried. I had to fight for my brother who was locked up and try to support him as much as I could, support my grieving mom and still be there for my own family. Then, of course, I had to try to help my siblings, especially the one who was there when it happened. We had to find some way to cope with our loss. It felt like someone came and snatched my breath away.

Oftentimes, I found myself fighting back the tears while I suffered internally in silence because I was on both sides of the table moving forward. Figuring out how to show unconditional love for one brother while trying to grieve another one and not come off as not caring about him was a pretty hefty task. I tried my best to prepare to go through the court process where it would be justice for one brother and me helping to defend another brother, so his life was spared. There would be absolutely no win here. Most of the time, I spent time fighting the thoughts and visions of the entire situation. I didn't know whether to punch something, kick, or scream. I walked around numb, confused, angry, heartbroken, and wondering why I didn't just stop and call them that day.

Only the grace of God could give me what I needed to make it through such a tumultuous time. Every day, I tried to talk to God but was unable to utter the right words. I could see the words in my mind, but they never rolled off my tongue. I could feel them in my heart, but nothing was being released. Most times I would open my mouth to pray and all I could say was, 'Jesus.' I would just sit there and stare at the walls, but nothing else would come out. I wanted to pray but couldn't. My hope was that God heard my silent prayers and honored the strength it took to just call the name of Jesus. It was no time not to pray, but I just couldn't do it. My insides cried out to God without speaking a single word. That would be the fight of my life.

The next week came and all arrangements were being finalized. My brother didn't have insurance, so we had to pay out of pocket, but we got it done. Sadly, there was very little outside support from family members. No one could have ever told me that I would be in that situation. My husband took on the responsibility of going down to the coroner to view the body, getting his clothes together and dealing with the funeral home so I didn't have to. There was no way I could handle seeing him in a cold morgue. He was only twenty years old. So much life yet to live and I didn't want that to be the last image I had of him.

We had secured everything and the last thing to do was pay for my brother's plot and money was running short. My husband had taken money from our savings for all the other arrangements and we were still short. I had been holding on to a check and decided I would use that to cover the expense. Usually, when I put a check in the bank it clears right away but of course when I really needed it something happened. I went to the bank and told the teller to just cash the check and give me a money order payable to Mt. Hope

Cemetery. As I stood there anxiously waiting for the money, I saw her hesitantly turn to me and say, "I'm sorry, there will be a 5-day hold on the check." I knew I didn't have enough in my account to take out what I needed.

Tears started to fall. I cried to her, "Please can you do something? My brother died and I don't have the money to pay to bury him and his funeral is in 2 days. We can't wait 5 days." She fought back tears and she tried to calm me down and turned to someone who directed her to one of the other bankers sitting in the lobby. Overwhelmed and crying, I prayed. *Dear God, please I need this money.* I sat there nervously as the guy pecked the letters on his keyboard. He finally turned to me and directed the teller to give me the cashier's check made payable to the funeral home.

I can't imagine how it looked. I was an unstable mess and filled with so many emotions that they probably thought I was crazy. I just needed to make sure there were no delays and that my brother was laid to rest peacefully. I mean, I would hope no one would try to defraud a bank asking for a cashier's check to a funeral home. Finally, I had my check in my hand and I hurried to the car because I was en route to the funeral home.

I remember having to choose a plot for him with my mom and feeling like I wanted to pass out. As we drove through the cemetery, they drove us to the back of Mt. Hope and I cried. No, I wasn't going to allow them to bury him all the way in the back. Once we stopped at a plot, I told the worker my concerns and he said, "Ma'am these other plots are more expensive." Again, I burst out crying explaining to him that this was my younger brother and that I needed him to be closer to the front. He looked around and found a space that would be okay under the circumstances. When we got out of the car to walk to the area, pure shock overtook me as I stood there. *I cannot believe that is honestly happening. We are burying him. This will be his final resting place. Dear God.*

The eerie feeling of standing in that cemetery watching other families who were there to bury their loved ones was one I just couldn't handle. The people were crying and watching the workers dig the plots where their family would be laid.

We finally got all the arrangements together and it was time to approve the body prior to the service. I was certain that was going to push me over the edge. As my husband drove me to the funeral home, my heart raced wondering if I could handle seeing my brother's dead body lying in a casket. We were nearing the end of the process, but I knew it was really just the beginning. *Jesus. I just want this nightmare to be over.*

Once we arrived, they led us into the room where he was. As I walked slowly up to the casket, tears flowed heavily from my face and my heart felt like it was in my shoes. He looked so handsome lying there with his arms folded as if he was only sleeping. The funeral home had done such a great job with him. He looked as if he was dressed and ready for prom. They had even trimmed him up to have a nicely trained beard that he never adorned while living. I just wished that he was really asleep and would wake up soon.

Come back home with big sister and let's just start this like it never happened. This shouldn't be real. You just spent the weekend at my house. Why didn't I just keep you there? I just stared at his lifeless body. Meanwhile, my chest was tight as if someone had loaded it with a ton of bricks. So many thoughts were rushing through my head. It was still impossible for me to process that as reality even as I watched him lie there.

My mind drifted off again to questions that no one seemed to have the answers to. I just couldn't stop wondering how any of it happened. Although I didn't have the answers that I was so desperately searching for, the whole thing explained the anxiety and uneasy feeling I had that Friday. It even explained why my baby was crying more than usual. Our spirits picked up on what was happening.

Could I have done anything? Should I have kept him with me instead of taking him back home? Was this all my fault? Could I have saved him from dying? Could I have stopped the fight? Maybe I should have called my mom's house to see what was going on that day. Why didn't I just have the urge to call? Had I been too busy with work that day when God was warning me? Did I ignore Him nudging me to pay attention? Could I have prevented this? So many questions. So many what ifs. The questions wouldn't stop and drove me crazy. That was the continued turmoil I went through every day for a good while after his death. Maybe I couldn't save the world, but just maybe I could have saved my brother.

For months, I played back the day of his death in my head and tried to imagine how it all happened. I never truly figured it out, but I felt crushed each time. I blamed myself because after all I was the older sister and they looked up to me. I had always looked out for them. An immense feeling of failure came over me. *He should have stayed with me longer and he would have probably still been alive today. I wouldn't be here now making funeral arrangements, or our other brother wouldn't be in jail. We wouldn't be tormented by the thoughts of how he died.* The grief was unbearable.

There was already so much pressure on me without me adding to it but at the time I wasn't thinking straight. I'm not God and I can't control everything that happens. I couldn't save the world even though I always felt like I wore a bright red cape with a big "T" tied around my neck. I was the big sis. Tasha was the protector in their eyes, the person they looked up to and I missed an opportunity to come and catch the fall. I didn't come and save the day. Or their lives. It's how I felt. Whether right or wrong, it's how I felt.

All arrangements were in place and it was just a matter of time until the day came that this new reality would set in. I'd have to come to terms with the fact that he did indeed die. I would have to come to grips with the fact that my brother really passed away and the circumstances surrounding it. It didn't matter that we went through the process of planning a funeral, picking plots, making sure his clothes were together or finalizing the church. Walking in and seeing him lying in a casket was just something I could not wrap my mind around.

The morning of the service came. It was a gloomy and cloudy day. My house was so quiet and somber. We all got dressed and waited in silence for the car to take us to the church. Each one of us quietly tried to save our energy to get through the day ahead of us. There were no conversations, just forced smiles here and there. On our ride to the service, it started to drizzle. It seems like every time someone dies and it's their day to be laid to rest, it's rainy and cloudy outside.

As we rode to the church, I couldn't help but think about my incarcerated brother. The guilt and shame he had been feeling would probably have been intensified if he knew that we were headed to his brother's service. Lorenzo wasn't here anymore, and my other brother was facing the rest of his life in jail. I imagined that he must have really been going through as he sat in jail uncertain about his future. He was not even able to attend the service and say goodbye or make his peace with Lorenzo. Perhaps he wanted to apologize for what happened or stand before him asking God for forgiveness. Something so unimaginable happened in our family and the family tree had forever been broken.

Due to the nature of what happened, he didn't come to the service. He didn't want to be a distraction nor show up shackled in handcuffs with correctional officers behind him. I knew that I would not be able to handle that nor anyone else. I also didn't want anyone shouting out any harsh words to him either. People were angry, hurt and some didn't have the relationship with God to be able to try and see the bigger picture or just weren't in a place yet to even think of forgiving him. I couldn't expect anyone to have the compassion that I had at the same moment that I had it. Everyone arrives in their own timing and it wasn't my place to say how they should or shouldn't act or what they should or shouldn't do.

Yet, I still wondered how he was being treated there. *What were the next steps in dealing with what lies ahead of him? How would my family deal and get through this? How do we even begin to get over this? Is that even possible to do?* So many emotions, so much hurt, so much trauma. My heart just ached to its core. I experienced deeply rooted hurt like I had never felt in my entire life; I never even knew a hurt like that existed. It was such a terrible spot to be in and I wouldn't wish it on any family.

We finally arrived at the church and as we walked in the minister began to recite Psalms 23:4. "Though I walked through the valley of the shadow of death…" I just lost it. Tears leaked from my eyes as I passed my brother's casket to go to the family's seating area. *Twenty years old with a whole life ahead of him. Look at him so peaceful looking dressed in his suit with his facial hair trimmed so neatly. Hands folded. So handsome.* He didn't look dead to me. I know it may sound crazy, but I wanted to yell at him up and say, 'wake up.' *Wake up! This is all just a terrible dream. This shouldn't be us and he shouldn't be here.*

Well, that day would prove that it wasn't a dream. It was real and the service made it more real than ever. It was the last time I would be able to see him on this earth. We finalized everything about that moment I had been dreading the whole week. *Jesus, help me!* He really was gone, and we would never see him again. He would never come to my house and eat seconds at Thanksgiving and load up on my dressing he loved so much. My baby would never know his uncle. He would never play games or ball with my children. It was never going to happen. All we would have were memories.

People began to file into the church and the service began. It was overwhelming for us. All the cries, screams and sadness made me feel like I couldn't breathe. *Hyperventilating.* The church was packed with people and if it was any comfort during such a tragic time, it was evident that people truly loved him. So many spoke good things about him.

My brother was very quiet and introverted like me. If you didn't bother him, he didn't bother you. We never had any trouble from him. *What happened here? Siblings fight, but why was this time so different?* The mere thought of wondering what his last moments were like hurt me so badly. I didn't know all the details of what happened other than his last words were, "I don't want to die," before he passed away in my other brother's arms.

It crushed me. I pray that he had enough energy to ask God to save him again. He had before but I wanted to take some type of comfort that God had him. There were so many thoughts going through my mind as I watched him lie there that I wasn't sure how to channel so many emotions and still be strong for everyone else. I did my best to hold it together, but I couldn't. It hurt like hell and there was nothing that could make it go away.

Out of routine, you often hear people say they understand but you don't if you've never personally experienced that type of trauma. People meant well but *sorry* or any of the other words spoken wouldn't reverse this tragedy and breathe life back into him. *Sorry* was not going to release my brother from jail. *Sorry* wouldn't heal my mom's wounded heart from the pain of a child dying. Kids weren't supposed to die before parents. *Sorry* couldn't erase the replaying of the event in my brother's eyes as he struggled to move forward or any of my other siblings who were just trying to navigate their way to finding coping mechanisms.

At some points in the service it felt like I was there but not there. My physical body was there but my mind was still racing with so many thoughts and emotions. I just felt numb and angry at times that the enemy had come in and caused destruction. My body was also tired from going nonstop since everything happened. It was almost as if I couldn't stop moving for fear of breaking down if I stopped. So, sitting in the service caused a lot of uncontrollable thoughts.

I couldn't stop my mind from traveling from one thing to the next as we sat and listened to the minister finish the service. When they rolled my brother's casket by the family for the last time, I wanted to clench my fist together like from the scene of *Good Times* when Florida lost it. There's no other way I can explain it.

The minister ended with a prayer and as the family got up to leave the building, I walked with my head hanging low trying not to make eye contact with any of the people who attended the service. I just didn't have the energy to interact with anyone or hear another *sorry* and my introverted personality didn't like crowds much.

That was the first time someone close to me passed away. It was going to take all my strength and God to get me through. *This is only part of the process.* Next, I would begin the journey of helping to save the life of my incarcerated brother. Not to mention, I had no idea where to even begin or how the court process would work.

But that was me always thinking into the future. I sat there with the heaviest burden I'd ever felt in my life all while not taking my eyes of Lorenzo because that was it. It was our final goodbye and soon after, life would require a

Tasha I didn't know I could be. I knew I had a long road ahead with having to deal with what this did to the other brother and how we could help him. It was a road I had never traveled or ever thought I could travel. The mere thought of being in the middle put even more stress on me. The defendant would be my brother and on the other side I'd be facing a prosecutor that would fight like hell for justice for my other brother. Of course, under different circumstances I would be the one on the other side fighting for my deceased brother.

We headed to the cemetery for the final goodbye. My family quietly got into the car and rode to Mt. Hope Cemetery where he would have his resting place. Once we arrived and the family was out, the minister began to speak and as he lowered my brother's casket in the ground, we each silently said our goodbyes and dropped a flower on his casket. It was the most devastating conclusion to a dreadful experience. *This boy really died, and our brother is really accused of his death. Damn, damn, damn.*

When we arrived home after the repast, a few of his friends and family members came over to keep my mom company and thankfully they did because all I could do was crawl upstairs to my bedroom to shower and lie down. Mentally exhausted from the day, I tried to get some rest, but the phone rang putting my rest on hold. It was my incarcerated brother on the other end. His voice was so low. You could hear the pain in his voice and shame as he began to ask me how the service was. He went on to say that he was so sorry and wanted to come but he didn't know how people would react. He only wanted to let our brother have a service without issues of him being there. He was fully aware that no one wanted him around and he knew that it would be trauma for him too.

    I comforted him the best way I could with the little energy I had left from the day. I mustered up just enough strength to tell him how things went. It seemed and sounded so strange talking about it with him. There was really nothing left in me from the day and I pretty much had not rested well or slept much since everything happened. So, I told him I loved him, and we would talk later. I knew my brother was scared and didn't know what his future held for him. He had been charged with first degree murder. Imagine that. Charged with killing your brother. It was heart wrenching.

    Lying in the bed, I desired to talk to God but was still unable to gather up the strength to even begin telling Him how I felt or asking Him for what I needed. If you've experienced any type of trauma, maybe you can relate. I know I needed God and I knew only He could take something so tragic and turn it around, but how? It wasn't going to bring Lorenzo back. I didn't know how, but I knew that God wasn't going to leave me in this alone. He couldn't because there was no other way I could make it.

Looking back, so much came at me from all directions that it felt suffocating to say the least. I was married with three young kids and running a home business. I was always doing what I could to be the light and help where and when I could. From accepting my incarcerated brother's calls a couple times a week trying to help encourage him to sending and writing countless letters to keep his spirits lifted to never missing a court date. He had become my personal prison ministry. On top of all of that, I was still worried about the other brother who witnessed everything. Clearly, he was struggling with it, but he would always just say, "I'm okay Tasha." However, the mother in me saw otherwise.

Watching my mom and sister trying to cope along with two other brothers weighed heavily on my spirit. Being a mother myself, I couldn't possibly imagine what my mom must have been going through. A child shouldn't go before the parent and in this case, it was even harder due to the circumstances surrounding it. All and all, I just kept going full speed ahead. There was never really a chance to do a self-check to see if I was okay. I had no time for that. There was a mission to accomplish and I had to make sure my mom didn't lose another son and we didn't lose another brother. The idea of that and the enemy winning was not going to happen. It would be like him getting the victory and there was no way I would let that happen.

It was just a lot. But God! One thing I always knew was that no matter what I had lean into Him. Some days I couldn't pray but I learned enough growing up from going to church with my grandma and being in Sunday school. All you sometimes needed to do was call on Jesus. I knew God heard my cries and that sometimes just uttering His name was enough. He knew exactly what I was facing and cared for each of us. Just the name gave me enough strength to push a little more when the prayers wouldn't come out. However, at some point I knew that I would need to do more than just say Jesus because there was a huge fight ahead of me.

Through all of that, I continued to go about life the best way I knew how because things continued to move for sure. Time waits for no one and it doesn't matter what you deal with in this life. Good or bad you must roll with the punches, get back up and prepare for the next fight. My life always seemed to be a fight here and there. Having been abused mentally and physically by my mom's ex-preacher husband to watching him abuse my siblings and then my mom was indeed a fight. But that's another story.

So, if nothing else I knew how to push through and persevere. I knew how to fight and survive.

It's life and it happens to all of us in different ways and on various journeys. We all walk a different walk. This happened and we were all dealing with it in our own ways and learning to press on. No matter how hard the fight or press was, we only had two options. Get knocked down and stay down or get up and continue to fight. Fight is what I did. It's what I always knew to do, and God carried me then and he was carrying me now.

If you've lived long enough then you know life doesn't stop when bad things happen, and you just get through it one day at a time. I still found a way to continue going to see my grandmother and dropping her groceries off like I usually would. I was extremely close with her and would always stop over to make sure she had food in her fridge. She had a few health conditions but was still healthy enough to move around. Encouraging and caring for others has always come naturally to me. I guess that's a part of the older child syndrome. No matter what was going on, I wanted my close loved ones to be okay and my grandmother was my heart.

I spent most days juggling motherhood, running my business, trying to do normal everyday life things, and going to visit my brother in jail as often as I could. It was never easy, but I found my own ways of coping and continuing with life one day at a time. Most days I wondered how I even made it when I felt so emotionally, mentally, and physically depleted from pouring out so much to others. One thing I've always known about myself is that I had the ability to encourage even when I wasn't feeling encouraged myself. Doing so made me feel better in some strange way. I'm sure it's because most times I shared things that I probably needed to hear myself.

ROUND TWO

Fighting for Life

Fight the good fight of faith.
—1 Timothy 6:12 NIV

My personal family was thriving. We were preparing to move into a house that we had the pleasure of watching being built from the ground up. I made sure to take the kids over at each phase just so that we could do things that felt normal again. Normalcy was good. We were all moving along wonderfully. The kids were doing well, and we were all enjoying our new home. Even amidst tragedy, God was still taking care of me and supplying our family with blessings; I was more than grateful. My incarcerated brother began to adjust to prison life. My mom and sister were back at work and my other brother was doing his best to move on. He got a new job and rented an apartment not too far from me. For the most part, he seemed to be doing okay as can be expected on the surface and trying hard to find ways to cope, but deep down inside I felt that he really should have started a round of therapy. Honestly, all of us should have signed up. And don't think I didn't keep pushing him on it here and there. I did, but he would never accept. That never stopped me from trying though. I kept my eyes on him to ensure that he was good.

Through all my struggles I hadn't paid attention to myself as much as I could. At the end of the day, no matter what I went through or how much I was the go-to for everyone, my health was important and had been neglected far too long. My family had a history of high blood pressure and I was determined not to live that life on meds and there was no way I could do it for anyone if my health failed me. After a scare at the doctor being diagnosed with prehypertension, I had to get fit and start taking better care of me. I began finally making time to work on my health and fitness. Going to the gym regularly and eating better became a part of my regimen.

It was me-time after years of neglecting my health and things were under control. I started to lose some weight which caused me to want to acquire further knowledge. Going through all I had it was so needed and divine. I guess it showed so much that my daughter made a statement that I should teach fitness classes. That thought was immediately thrown out the window but when I was alone, I found myself thinking about it. *Why not?* That outlet was right on time when I needed it the most; I was looking forward to trying something new. I decided to register for school to become a certified personal trainer.

Even though I had inquired about school months prior, I really hadn't gotten serious about it until my little divine intervention happened with the help of my daughter. Afterwards, my husband followed me down to get registered. The thought of starting school was so intimidating to me, but it all worked out. One of my friends had kids that attended the same school as mine and she agreed to take them and pick them up Monday through Thursday while I attended classes. I was in class from 8 am until 3 pm. It was a win-win situation, and I was off to start a new journey. The downtime of my daily train commute and a few hours of quiet time was welcomed and enjoyed.

But then out of nowhere, I was dealt another blow. It was as if life was just too calm that the adversary had to come wreck our peace. One weekend I was at home preparing to visit my grandma when I received a call from my aunt that my grandma wasn't conscious. I knew she had been in the hospital. We talked multiple times a day. Our last conversation was her telling me not to come to the hospital and to wait and save the visit for the house. She reassured me that the doctors just wanted to do one more test but that she was feeling fine and would see me over at the house later. Apparently, they decided to do an angiogram, and something went wrong but nobody knew exactly what. All we knew is that she was unable to speak.

I got in my car and drove to the hospital not knowing what to expect when I got there. When I walked in her room, I found her just lying there non-responsive to me being there or calling her name. I was standing over my grandmother who I just adored. She always did anything for me. That crushed me. I couldn't believe that we had just spoken about me visiting her. She insisted that I should just wait and come over to her house. She said it was fine and the test was no big deal. She assured me but I found myself wishing I'd just gone to the hospital anyway.

When I arrived and saw her unable to speak, I was angry and wanted answers. Once again, my spirit felt uneasy at the hospital and I wasn't feeling great vibes from the hospital staff about exactly what happened and why my grandmother unable to speak. Many of them kept going around in circles talking and I knew somebody was lying and holding back somewhere. I did not play about her! I wasn't the only one who sensed that something was not right. Other family members started to feel the same thing. Something truly felt amiss. What were they not saying? You don't go down for a test and come back unable to talk.

Here we go again. Life threw me another unexpected blow when I was at a place where things were finally settling down a bit from the earlier tragedy with my brothers. Now, we were there. That was my grandma and it hurt on a whole new level. She was my confidant, my best friend, my protector, and grandmother all rolled into one and she was lying there incapable of speaking to tell us what happened that caused her to land in that position.

My grandfather and uncle arrived at the hospital and both were looking for answers. After feeling like they were pulling teeth, someone finally said that she had a bleed after the angiogram where they go in through the groin. For the most part, it's supposed to be a simple procedure. The doctor is guided by a light to ensure that he's on the right poking path. She had gone through this procedure before and for the life of us we all couldn't understand what went wrong that time. All I know is that she was in that hospital bed unable and too weak to utter one word.

After weeks of no change, they inserted a tracheotomy in. We all spent as much time at the hospital as we could so she wouldn't be there much alone. We took different shifts, but there was no change in her condition. I spent countless visits watching her nurse come in and check her tracheotomy. I hated that thing. I hated how her heavy-handed nurse would come in while I was there just pushing the thing back and forth so aggressively and seeing my grandmother gag. Hell, she couldn't talk but we knew she heard us and still had feelings. Every time I watched her go through that I cringed. Every time I watched her do it, tears would well up in my eyes. I couldn't stomach someone inflicting pain upon her. She was hurting her and when I couldn't stand to watch any longer, I told her to take it easy. *Why is she being so aggressive?* Her response was, "Oh, she doesn't feel this." *How do you know she didn't feel it? Haven't they done enough to her?*

My uncle got into it with the nurse so badly that she was transferred to another part of the hospital. She told my uncle that she had seen patients like my grandma in her many years of nursing and that she wouldn't come out of something like that at her age. *Really?!* We as a family unit may have lacked a lot, but one thing we did have was faith. One person we wouldn't stand for anyone hurting was Lillie Mae, nor would we tolerate anyone speaking negatively over her when it appeared the reason that she was in that condition was because of the hospital.

The weeks kept passing by and I was pretty much driving to the south side from the suburbs every day or every other day to be by her side. I found myself once again trying to juggle family life and being there for my best friend, my grandmother. Day after day passed by and still zero change. We would see her fingers moving and grateful for some sign of hope only to have that hope shot down by the negative Nancy nurses caring for her. We tried so hard to keep it cool since they were the people who we had to trust to care for her when we all left.

With no real answers as to what caused it, we were all growing impatient watching her unable to speak and tell us what happened. They had inserted a tracheotomy and ran countless tests. That's all we knew. And they were still jerking us around with no real answers or answers that sat right with us. My grandfather, who was due to pick her up the day she was supposed to be discharged, recounted how he called the hospital for hours and she never answered her phone. He was trying to see if the "simple" procedure was over so he could pick her up.

Time continued to pass, and she wound up having to get another tracheotomy inserted because the one they inserted earlier became infected. They were putting her through so much added pain. She couldn't tell us what hurt. She jumped here and there and moved her fingers continually, but that's all we saw. *What have they done to my sweet grandmother?* It was killing me inside to see her that way. I wished I had just come the day of the procedure when she was due to be released. Somebody should have been there with her.

She had been given the papers to be released when they came in and informed her that they wanted to do one more thing before she left. So, she called her husband and told him not to come for discharge just yet. Everyone was under the impression that she was fine and her initial admittance for diabetes issues were under control again after the three-day stay. No one expected them to do an angiogram. *Why didn't they wait for someone to be here with her or even call us?*

At one point, we were all coming and going at unlimited times to be there waiting and praying for some sign of hope and relief. Sadly, we saw none and started to get impatient and demanded a family meeting with all involved in her care. That's when we finally heard from her personal doctor who treated her outside of the hospital that it was indeed medical malpractice. Words from a medical doctor himself that she had gone for the test and the machine that allowed them to see where they were poking had gone out, not one time. Not two times. But three freaking times! The doctor kept going instead of stopping the test after the first poke when it went out. Who does that? But that was just the beginning of their negligence.

After the test, she was wheeled back up to her room. My grandmother was in her seventies. No one came to see about her in a timely fashion, and when they did my sweet dear grandmother was bleeding from where they went in during the angiogram. The nurse didn't even realize what happened until after calling out asking my grandmother's name to see if she was okay. She was practically non-responsive and when she pulled the covers back to check the area of insertion she was bleeding heavily. The bed sheets were soiled, and she was bleeding so much that the nurse panicked and left a seventy-something-year-old woman to apply pressure to her own wound. *Are you kidding me?* She was an elderly woman who I'm sure was weak and even weaker after the procedure. How do you even fix your mouth to instruct her to apply pressure to her bleeding side? By herself? And she's unresponsive?

Why would the nurse leave her bedside and not use the call button at the side of her bed to get additional help? *Why would you leave the room?* That was totally unprofessional and unacceptable. She was supposedly a registered nurse who should have been trained to handle a situation like that much better. However, she panicked and just about left her to die and bleed to death. That explained why she was unconscious. She had lost so much blood during the whole experience. Once they finally got it under control, it was too late. Though alive, she was semi-unconscious.

I prayed so hard every day hoping she would get better and so did the rest of the family. Days, weeks, and months went by. She was transferred to this hospital and that hospital across Chicago and still no change. Family meeting after family meeting with doctors until eventually the last hospital she was transferred to told us that she would not recover. The damage had been done and they were giving her six months or less to live.

There we were listening to a doctor flat out tell us that I was about to lose my grandmother forever. *Is he crazy? Does he know how much I love this woman and how I can never accept this type of news. What does he mean six months or less? Is he*

God? That was my heart. I couldn't fathom the idea of her not being around. We talked every single day, multiple times a day. She was the woman who helped raise me, fought for me, showered me with gifts and money, and lived to see me have children and get married. *And you're telling us she's as good as dead?*

No, I wouldn't accept it. There was no way on this earth I could be without her. My grandfather kept repeating, "But she moved her hands! Didn't you see her?" What the doctor said went in one ear and right out the other with him. If he saw her fingers moving, he said there was still hope and we were not about to even consider giving up. The doctor responded that her finger movement was not really her doing; it was just her reflexes. My grandfather didn't accept that it was just a natural response. Yet, her condition was still in fact her condition.

The words that the doctor had just spoken were grime. Each family member that stood in the meeting room looked so bewildered and completely out of it. We looked at each other with the look of terror at the words just spoken about our beloved Lillie Mae. The matriarch of the family. Absolutely no way. She was fighting and we would fight too.

My grandmother was a fighter. She had overcome many things and I knew she was fighting her way back. I believed God. Yes, I was thankful for doctors, but I believed God and that is what I held onto. No way was I going to let her go. During that whole sad experience, they transferred her to at least four hospitals, but she continued to fight so giving up was no option.

    She remained at the last hospital for weeks until there was another meeting and that time the conversation was about hospice. The hospital had given up and by that time, her care bill was at least $500,000, if not more and she had Medicaid. They told the family they had done all that they could and at that point we needed to just let her go. Let her go peacefully and release her so she wouldn't suffer any longer.

    The family reluctantly agreed on hospice, but we still believed that God could do miracles and we prayed and believed it for her. She was a fighter, and we were going to continue to fight for her until her last breath. We were not about to give up. She was the rock of the family. She loved to cook and have people over until she had gotten up in age and could no longer handle it. I just couldn't give up on her. My children adored her as much as I did. The youngest child would always play games with her. That was their special little bond. There were so many precious moments and the medical team told me that me, nor my children would live those moments again.

I'm reminded that around Easter she prepared her last big dinner and had everyone over, but I didn't attend because I was going through something at home. My aunt said at one point she got a chair and sat it in the middle of the floor in the living room where everyone was gathered dressed in all white. My aunt mentioned how she had watched her eating like it was her last meal. *Did she have a feeling that God was about to call her home?* I had a feeling one morning when my husband was getting dressed for work. All I remember is that I jumped up from sleep with my ear ringing and said someone is going to die, not knowing that it would be her.

Once again, I was facing another tragedy with additional trauma and it was really going to hit in a different way. Although she was resting comfortably in hospice, my heart couldn't take much more. *Did God think I was strong? Did He think I could handle all this?* I was still supporting my incarcerated brother who occasionally had bad days that I had to talk him through. Honestly, I don't know how I mustered up the strength to keep pouring out and being so much to everyone, but some way God always gave me the extra push I needed when I needed it. But dealing with my grandmother, I felt I had reached my limit. *This is my heartbeat. My grandma.*

My time was spent day in and day out worrying about my brother, sitting by my grandmother's bedside talking to her, and trying to figure out how I was going to handle losing her all while going through things at home. *This hurts deeply and God is going to have to do a miracle here.* Seriously, I felt like I was losing it. *How much more can one person take? I am not perfect, but I consider myself a pretty good human being with a good heart. Why is God allowing this to happen? Was I some terrible human being in the past life? Someone please make me understand. Understand how I am dealing with trauma on a level I had never seen or experienced.*

    The hospice continued to do all they could to make her comfortable. It was so hard going there day after day hearing the cries of people in pain. Here and there, I witnessed the pain faced by families as their loved ones died. We found ourselves dreading that same pain as we were told to anticipate the death of my darling grandmother. We were told that too would be our fate and to prepare ourselves for it at any moment, any given day. *How do you prepare?* I wasn't ready and didn't know how to prepare for death. Yes, I had gone through my brother's tragic death, but that was a new type of trauma. It was different from before with an all new level of mind-blowing circumstances surrounding it. *How am I going to handle it when that time comes? Dear God, please do something!*

Most times, my drive home was in silence praying and begging God to please not take her away from me. Growing up, I always prayed for God to allow her to live to see me grow up and have children of my own. When I remembered what I prayed, I went back to Him to revise the prayer. *Please give her a long life to see my children grow up.* All I know is I needed her here with me on this earth.

How can I ever explain this to my kids? My daughter loved to go to her house and indulge in the great breakfast that nobody could do like great grandma. She must have kept every single picture that I had given her of my oldest son. The collection included pictures from the womb until his current age. She had picture albums that were all his own. Then there was my youngest who used to have staring contests with her and tried his hardest not to lose but could never master how not to let grandma win. He would ask her to turn her face and rub his cheeks as if when they started the contest again that would help him. It never did. He would always burst into laughter with that cute little face. Those were the precious moments I would never feel again.

How was I going to tell them that the great grandma that they loved so much passed on? My heart couldn't handle what I was about to face. *How can one ever prepare for death and in this case the trauma that came with it?* She hadn't gone peacefully. She suffered six long, agonizing months. Heck, I hadn't fully recovered from the trauma of my brother's death or the situation surrounding it and life dealt me another loss. Another trauma. Pain on top of pain.

Still in all, I never for once stop believing that God could give us a miracle for her. I was just wired that way. She was worth fighting for until the end and I wasn't about to give up on her.

By that time, I was dibbling and dabbling in real estate as well. One morning I planned out my day and wanted to go to the hospital after a meeting, but something told me not to. I knew that feeling all too well. So, when the Holy Spirit spoke, I listened to the nudging. As clear as day, I heard God say, "Go to the hospital first," so I rearranged my schedule and did just that. *The kids get out of school at 3:00 and I can make it back to the 'burbs to get them in time.* I am so glad I followed the Spirit's lead that day.

Upon arrival at the hospital, I had to pass the nurses' station to get to her room. When I walked in, one of the nurses greeted me and said, "Oh, hi. Your grandmother is doing so well today." Now that was a first because they were never that jolly when I came in. *Something is definitely up.* She stated how bright and glowy her skin looked. Although I loved hearing that news, my spirit spoke something else. *Dear God...NO!*

As I walked into her room, there she lay facing the window looking so beautiful and peaceful. Her beautiful brown skin radiant as ever and her wavy hair caressed against her face perfectly. It was sunny that day and there was a ray of sun that beamed down on her glowing skin just as the nurse had described. She looked so at rest; the room had a different vibe that day. In a crazy way, there was a level of comfort moving throughout the room. It had a different ambience.

The presence in the room didn't feel as heavy as it usually did. Everything was so serene. The atmosphere was filled with some type of feeling that even the words I've used to describe it don't do it any justice. The experience I had was of something so strong I'm unable to convey it. It was beautiful. Deep down inside, I kind of knew what was happening but wanted to dismiss it. I wasn't ready to accept it. To be truthful, I wanted to lose it, but the atmosphere of the room kept me from breaking down. God's presence was there with my sweet grandma.

I pulled up a chair near her bedside to hold her and caress her hair. Most days when I showed up for a visit, I was never there alone but that day I was. No family members had come yet, and it was just her and me. My sweet beautiful grandma. The first time during a six-month fight, we were alone. God set that encounter up so perfectly as only a loving God could do.

As I sat near her bedside, I began to tell her how much I deeply loved her and couldn't begin to imagine my life with her not in it. I shared how she was always in my heart. How she was and always will be my heart and nothing or no one would ever change that. As tears began to stroll down my face, immediate grief encompassed me as I prepared myself for what I felt was about to happen. I continued pouring my heart out to her and I knew she could hear me. All I wanted to do was love her.

There was a moment of complete silence where I continued to squeeze her hand tightly, never wanting to let go or envisioning living in this world without my grandma. My heart just broke as I stroked her hands. I stood up to hug her and told her that she would always hold a special place in my heart as I placed her hand where she could feel it beating in my chest. *You will never die because you will continue to live in me. I know you are tired of fighting. I am tired of watching you suffer; you don't have to fight anymore. I am angry at what they have done to you. You certainly didn't deserve this, but I know God will take care of it. We never wanted to let you go, but if God is calling you, we will be okay. I want you here with me, but God has a much better place prepared for you awaiting your arrival.*

Those were the hardest words I have ever had to utter out my mouth, but I couldn't let her leave this earth without making my peace. God allowed us that special time and I will cherish it for the rest of my life.

Time seemed to be moving so fast that day and anytime I visited, especially on school days, I had to factor in the time it would take to drive back to the suburbs to pick up the kids. That day I wished I had someone who could have picked them up for me, but I didn't. Of all the days there was no one. Knowing it would be my last time seeing her, I cried and loved on her down to the very last second that I could without risking being late to get the kids. When I couldn't spare any more time, I said my final goodbye to her filled with tears and uncontrollable grieve.

The harder I tried to leave, the harder it felt like something was pulling me not to, but I had to go. I kept creeping toward the door inch by inch wanting to savor every moment of our time together. *This is going to be the last time I will be alone with her. That nudging this morning was God preparing me. He set it up so we could have our moments together. Just the two of us.*

Time was ticking and as I slowly approached the door, I turned to tell her that I was so sorry to have to leave. *Please know I love you with all my heart.* When I looked back at her as I approached the door, I saw tears streaming down my grandmother's face. It crushed my entire soul. I knew she heard me, and I believe she made peace with God and was ready to stop fighting.

    In tears, I walked to my car. That same agitation I felt when my brother passed away was the same feeling I felt as I drove to get the kids. I knew that feeling all too well. When I got the kids, it got stronger and stronger and I cried all the way home. I tried my hardest to fight the tears and make it home, but I couldn't. My babies looked so sad because they knew grandma was ill, but they were too young to understand just how much. No words could ever explain my love for that woman. Once again, I was facing the trauma and grief of a loved one. I had gone from never losing anyone that close to me to losing two.

    The kids and I finally arrived at home and I had just sat down at my kitchen table when my phone rang. It was my aunt on the other line and all she said was, "Tasha, she's gone. She's gone." She took one big breath and peacefully passed on. God allowed us our alone time and she continued waiting for her children to arrive to see her one last time and took her last breath. I'm so happy I was able to have that time and if anything, there was comfort in knowing that she heard me and knew how I felt about her. We had to let her go and allow her to stop fighting which I know she did down to the very last minute.

I literally just broke down and cried as I ran upstairs to check the house phone to see if I had saved any messages on my phone from her. I needed to hear that calming voice she would always leave on my phone if I missed her call.

My aunts and everyone stayed at the hospice unit until the coroner arrived which was hours later. I wanted so much to run back to the hospital to see her just one more time and wait with them, but they talked me out of it. She had passed away from this earth and I felt like my world just stopped. It was unbearable. I knew it was never realistic to think she would always be on this earth, but the selfish part of me just wanted her here as long as I could have her. It brought me so much joy to see her interact with my children, but God called her home. My sweet dear grandma was at rest with the Lord. No more pain and suffering.

A couple of days passed and still shaken by her death, the family prepared for the service. Her service would be held at the church that her late brother pastored and the church I grew up going to with her on Sundays. That was one time I wasn't tasked with making the funeral arrangements and I'm glad because I didn't think I could handle that one. I found a special poem to add to her obituary and ordered flowers.

Everything was complete and the day of service came and just like the morning of my brother's service everyone was again somber, and I was not looking forward to the day ahead of me. When the family arrived at the church, her car was already there parked just outside the door. I couldn't believe my sweet angel had left me. *How am I going to go on?*

After a few moments, we walked up the stairs to church to find seating and as I sat down my legs began to shake. My whole inside was shaking. As the service went on, it got worse and my husband reached over to put his hand on me to try to control it, but it didn't help. My body was traumatized. *Here I am again facing the death of a close loved one. And even after this, another new phase will begin because there is no way my family is allowing the hospital and all involved to get away with killing my grandma. She didn't deserve to suffer how she did, and they are going to be held accountable.* But we had to lay her to rest first before we took any legal action.

I seriously needed God to carry me because the traumas of those deaths were starting to consume me, and I had to stay strong. That was one time I wasn't sure if I had any fight left in me and if I did, it sure didn't feel like I was going to win. From a young age, people always seemed to find comfort in opening up to me. No matter my age, I have always been the go-to person to talk to. The gift of encouragement and knowledge has always been very present in my life. My age never stopped me from being the strong one, but everything that transpired left the encourager tired and hurting inside.

All I really wanted was something to make everything go away but God continued to carry me all those days like He always has. Each time it felt like I couldn't go on, I silently prayed and cried, as I found myself struggling to find the words to express to Him. Yet, He always seemed to hold me and give me exactly what I needed to keep pushing. I am not sure why He felt that I had it in me, but He did, and He never let me fall.

Each trauma took a piece of me. I don't think anyone around me really understood the internal agony I was experiencing losing my grandmother. Most nights, I lied in bed silently crying and feeling lost. There were times that I would forget that she was gone and pick up the phone to call her. Then there were other times that I reflected on the many instances I would go places with her, and she would tell total strangers I was her daughter. She hardly ever referred to me as her granddaughter. So proud.

I recall those moments that I visited her at home, and she would stand at her door waving until the last minute she could see the car turn the corner. There was one time it happened, and it felt so final. I told my children that it made me feel some type of way. *Had God started preparing me and I just missed it?* When you have a deep bond with someone your spirit is sensitive, but I loved her so much that I never wanted to think of her not being around.

My world had been shattered into pieces. A part of me left when she died and though I had my family it was just different. The love for a grandma is just unexplainable. The void could never be filled. If there was a word stronger than love that's what I had for her. People always teased me because it was evident that I was her favorite and sometimes it felt like her daughters were jealous of the bond we shared. *How could I go on not hearing her voice everyday multiple times a day?* I missed her voice messages and listening to her calming voice over the phone. When I got married, she was happy and sad. Sadness came because she felt like my husband was taking me away from her, but happiness surfaced because she knew I was growing up and always told me how proud she was of me. Although, in her eyes, I was never really grown.

Sometimes she would call me and say I should come spend the night with her like I had always done, and I had to remind her that I was married. She would say, "So. Bring the husband and the kids with you." She didn't care; she just wanted me around. In her eyes I was always her little grandbaby. It was the most precious thing and I cherished every moment of life with her.

We had an unbreakable bond that left me totally distraught by her death. To this day, I haven't gotten over it and I don't think I ever will. As I pen this book, I can still feel the heaviness of sharing these experiences today.

To be totally honest, I'm not even sure I grieved her or my brother properly because I was always being the strong person for everyone else. Silently suppressing my feelings and doing my best to go on, I had people depending on me so there were no other options.

You never want to question God, but I just wanted to know why the blows were coming repeatedly, back to back. They didn't just die, they died tragically. What was God wanting to prove or build in me? Before getting out of one thing, another came. It was somewhat similar to Job in the Bible and how he kept losing and fighting a battle, all while questioning why.

As soon as things started to feel a little normal and allowed me the opportunity to start something new, it felt like I was stripped yet again. I was living in an emotional traumatizing experience that nobody could understand even if I tried to explain. I wasn't even sure I knew how to explain it. This debilitating hurt was way down deep and some way I had to learn how to fight through it. I had three amazing babies who needed their mommy.

Eventually, the family sought out an attorney and started the lawsuit. Some time went by before the actual trial started because the hospital refused to settle. Just as with my brother, I planned to be at every trial date and for the most part I was there all but one day. It was going to be two long, agonizing weeks listening to and seeing images. The hospital's job was to make the jurors think that my grandmother's health and health history led to her death when in fact it was the negligence on the hospital's part. I sat there listening to the hospital's attorney and honestly, I wanted to rip his neck off hearing him talk about her and her health ailments. But he had a job to do--save the hospital and keep the doctors from a death lawsuit.

I almost hated that attorney especially when he got cocky and said she was going to die anyway. *The absolute freaking nerve of this heartless bastard!* We gasped and I could see the reaction on the jurors' faces. They were very attentive and occasionally took notes. *Hopefully, they will see straight through the bull the attorney is feeding them.* The week went by and they rested their case and it was time for our side to present the following Monday.

The following week came, and we began to learn so much more than we knew as our side presented its case. There were so many painful details we didn't know about. It was unbelievable and hurtful to hear the amount of blood she lost during the minutes the nurse left her bedside. Some of it I just couldn't stomach. We also learned that due to negligence the second tracheotomy they inserted had gotten infected for improper cleaning. *Was this place a real hospital?* After what I observed, I wouldn't take a dog to that hospital.

We sat through so many exhibits and even listened to the testimony of her private doctor who testified. This is something that never happens. He knew the risks with testifying against the hospital, but he had been my grandmother's doctor for a while, and he cared for her as his patient. If it wasn't for his honesty, we probably would never know what they did to her because clearly their plan was to try and cover it up. Sitting through testimony after testimony was weighing on us all, and it was like another bad dream I was walking through yet again.

Our side wrapped up their arguments and the judge instructed that the following week would begin closing arguments. We felt that her attorney presented a strong case. It was clear they were negligent starting from the angiogram doctor right down to the nurses and tracheotomy doctor. So many people played a role in the fate of my grandmother taking a turn for the worse and I couldn't imagine the thought of them getting away with it. I prayed that the jurors took notes and could see straight through the ball of lies the hospital's attorney tried so eloquently to present. There was no way in my mind that anyone would believe him. No amount of money would be enough to bring her back, pay for her suffering or erase these memories we were forced to live with, but we still wanted to see justice served.

The week of closing arguments came, and we all went home awaiting the verdict. Well it didn't take long. The jurors deliberated for under 3 hours and came back with a guilty verdict and there you had it. Weeks of sitting through grueling testimonies were over. Some sense of closure came with the verdict, but it would never be enough. I just wanted my grandmother back. Life would never be the same without her.

The family was awarded a large sum of which the attorneys took half off the top. I am still unsure why his assistants were paid an equal amount and left the family of seven to split the leftovers, but that's another story. It also didn't seem right that she was awarded money for pain and suffering and the hospital that killed her was paid money for hospital bills. Yes, read that again. I was livid. They shouldn't have been given a dime. They were the reason we were even there. The reason I lost my sweet grandmother.

ROUND THREE

Fighting for Freedom

The only real prison is fear, and the only real freedom is freedom from fear.
—Aung San Suu Kyi

Some time went on and the process of deciding my brother's fate was upon us. The whole legal process was about to begin, and we got the first court date. That opened a whole other issue for me because I worked from home, had three young kids, and had to plan for them as I did what I could to help save this brother's life.

All my clients were scheduled around my brother's court dates. Every time they brought him out, I would be there. I can remember seeing him for the first time being called out. Shackled hands, feet, and waist. It made me cringe and he looked terrified trying so hard to hold it together. One thing he always did was turn around to see who was there in court for him. When I would walk in the courtroom the state's attorney always looked back at me. Then he would look to see who else was there. It didn't matter who was there when he saw me, he knew there was support. Court date after court date, I sat there by myself. It was a really lonely place to be in dealing with the whole process and knowing that it was due to the death of our brother.

We had never experienced anything like it, and I couldn't afford a criminal attorney, so we had to go the public defender route. When they called his name and he came out, I stood up. I wanted the judge to know he wasn't there alone. They needed to know that this wasn't going to be one with no family support. If I had to go at it alone, it was just what I would do. I didn't know how it would play out, but I knew God and I knew He would honor my sacrifices and see us through to the end. No way was I going to love God and not love my brother because of what had transpired. He wasn't a heartless killer.

He was my brother and we didn't have the best childhood. We were all physically, mentally, and emotionally abused as kids by my mom's husband who happened to be a preacher in the church. We witnessed domestic violence due to him. Once, we were awakened from our sleep to find out that he had stabbed my mom and caused her to get 44 stitches in her back. Most days, my brother didn't even go to school for fear of the gangs that were pursuing him for recruitment. No way I was going to let him go out like that. We did not have the easiest time coming up and it just didn't seem right to leave him to face that alone. His life was worth saving even if it meant I wouldn't have family support in court with me. Most of our lives we were raised by a single mom who worked long hours to take care of seven kids with no support. We were all we had, and I had always been there for them being the oldest. This situation wasn't going to change that. Why would I not fight to save his life knowing I had lost one brother who was never coming back.

It wasn't an excuse, but I was not about to leave him fighting alone and suffering for something he would have to live with for the rest of his life. I just couldn't bring myself to do it. As tragic as it was, it could have happened to any of us at any time. No one can ever say what they won't or can't do because the truth is we don't know unless we find ourselves in the situation. We pray it never happens to us, but you just never know.

That was a horrible position to be in because I never wanted it to seem like I was playing sides and loved my brother who died any less than this one. That could never be true. I loved them all the same and I realized my fight may sit well with some but when God places something on your heart you just do it. I was fighting a state's attorney who was in turn fighting for another brother whom I also loved. No one could ever know what type of burden that put on me, but I pushed through and did all I could. *I never asked to be put in this situation.*

It doesn't matter what other people say or how they feel, you must trust God. It won't be pretty all the time. Sometimes in life you may be forced to do things that people may not agree with. You just have to trust in what you believe and flow with it. I never wanted to hurt anyone. That wasn't the reason for standing so strong with him. All I know is that this was a horrible way to go out after all the things we all had faced, and I just would not stand by and do nothing.

Even though I was resolute in my stance regarding my supporting my brother, at some points I still felt guilty. I wondered what others thought about me supporting him. How did it make my mom feel? My other siblings? I didn't worry about my mom's side because I was used to them always having something to say so that didn't bother me.

It seemed like I was going to court for him every two weeks. It was rough with the kids and clients and still doing all I needed to do at home. I found myself more tired working from home than if I worked in the salon most days. But I had to keep pushing no matter how tired. Appearance after appearance, I always stood to show the judge and those who had my brother's fate in their hands that I was there in solidarity and support. One week, the state's attorney asked to speak with me and told me that I really didn't need to show up every single court date because the case would be continued every time until a plea deal was reached or my brother went to trial. He towered over me and in some way, I felt he was trying to intimidate me. *Good try.* I told him, "Don't worry. Every time you bring my brother out, I'll be sitting in the front row. But thanks for your concern." He snickered and walked away. *You will not intimidate me and besides, I know God got me!* I was depending on Him to direct my path and give me the strength to get through this.

Because we couldn't afford a criminal attorney, I made it my business to reach out to the public defender to make sure he knew who I was. I was good at researching and I spent a lot of time doing just that. I made sure the public defender had my number and would keep me informed about future court dates. He too would try to caution me about coming, but like I mentioned earlier, some way somehow God would make it possible to always be there. It took me being involved to push him to work because he knew I would be on him.

I think I became a pain in both their butts. I was always asking questions and challenging things that didn't sit right with me. I knew how public defenders worked but this was going to be different. I was on a mission to help save my brother. I had already lost one and why lose two if I could help it. Again, it didn't mean I didn't love my deceased brother, was playing sides or trying to be insensitive, although it may have felt that way to some. It also didn't mean that he was my favorite or anything. It just felt like it was the right thing to do.

Weeks and weeks went by and all they would do is continue the case. It was extremely tiring. Some days I didn't know if I was coming or going. It weighed me down and I know the only way I could have gotten through was by God's grace. It was mentally, physically, and emotionally draining every ounce of energy I had. Between court and taking my brother's calls, writing, and keeping money on the books, it was extremely taxing.

If you have ever had a painful experience of someone you know being in jail, you know that it can be very expensive and a complete emotional roller coaster. Some months I would have phone bills around $400, not to mention the money that I spent putting on his books. Some days he was up when he called. Some days down. I spent so many moments talking him through tough days and negative thoughts that would run through his mind. He worried if he would ever see light again and honestly, I didn't have the answer to that question. All I knew is that I was going to do my best to help him through this situation.

During this process I honestly ran myself ragged. Experiencing death isn't easy no matter how it happens, but under these conditions the mental toll it takes on your mind and body is unexplainable. I started developing bad headaches and had to get in to see my doctor and was warned that my blood pressure was borderline high and if it continued, I would need to start medication. That was not good news because it ran in my family and I was determined that it would not run with me.

The whirlwind that I was living in was unbelievable. *How do I manage to control my feelings at a time like this? So much is going on. I'm being pulled in so many directions. Still trying to grieve and process.* Honestly, I am not even sure I ever really grieved properly because I went directly into fight mode each time.

The fight was going to take everything I had to see it through to the end. It was a fight and I had no idea how it would turn out. But I believed God. I trusted Him. I knew He was with me but there was still that fear that likes to creep in. My brother was facing the reality of never seeing light again. First degree murder for killing of our brother. *30 years.*

The weeks continued to pass and court date after court date passed. It was like a cycle. He came out shackled, I stood with him and five minutes later he headed back to lock up. The hour drive it took me to get to court was summed up each visit by a five-minute continuation.

That was my routine for almost a year before I received a call from the state's attorney. The phone rang and I picked up to hear the words, "Tasha, we have reached a plea deal for your brother. I've already been down to the jail and discussed it with your brother, but he asked if I could also talk to you."

Omg! This is starting to move quicker now! As my heart raced, I hesitantly asked what the plea was. He said second degree murder. Seventeen years. I instantly shouted, "No! You can't do better than that?! He didn't mean to do it! He isn't the person you think he is. Please do something else!"

The state's attorney instructed me that if he didn't take the deal, he could face life. I am not even sure where the strength and courage came from, but I told him I would talk to my brother but doubted that he would be accepting that plea deal. Once again, he advised me that I really needed to talk to him and make sure he understood the severity of what he was facing. On one hand I understood, and on the other hand I also understood that God is and will always be a God of miracles.

Later that day when my brother called, we discussed it and he was scared and didn't know what to do. "Sis, I can't do 17 years. I just don't have it in me. I don't think I will survive." His voice was so low and depressed. He didn't want to accept the plea.

I hated the whole situation and the spot it put me in. The fight I was in to help save him didn't mean I didn't love my deceased brother, Lorenzo. His life was worth fighting for too. If the defendant was anyone but my brother, I know for sure that I would have still been in the courtroom fighting for Lorenzo and more than likely would have thought that 17 years was too little for his life. I would have been pushing for more years. There was no punishment enough for his life. Thus, I knew my brother would probably get some time, but 17 years was just too long.

Later that week I put a call into the public defender. I'm the type of person that researches a lot and if I believe in something I'm not backing down. I feel in situations like this, attorneys may work harder if they know that those incarcerated men aren't alone and have family support. By the end of our call, I think he knew I would probably be a thorn in his side until the case was settled.

The weeks continued to pass and anyone who has walked in my shoes and had an incarcerated loved one knows how grueling it can be. You don't just go to court for you, you sit there and hear everyone's case until your loved one is called. I was exhausted wondering when it would all end. *When will I know the fate of my brother?* The more it went on, the more I felt terrified for his future.

One Friday, I had one of my favorite clients in the chair and she noticed how quiet I was and wasn't my cheerful self. I explained what was going on and she suggested that I get everyone who knew my brother to sign a character petition. "Get something from his pastor and church. Have your mom write a letter and get it to the person over the state's attorney before the next court date."

God must have sent her because that was something that never crossed my mind to do. I wondered if my mom would be willing to write the letter. After all, I doubt she was at the forgiveness stage yet considering the reality of circumstances. She had just tragically lost a son. She had another one incarcerated. Then there was the weight that she carried knowing that a fight involving all three of her sons caused the entire ordeal. It was a lot. I couldn't expect people to act as I did. As much as I wanted them to, I could not expect everyone to forgive early and want to support him, but I was definitely going to try.

As the time continued to pass, it gave us room to get all the letters and signatures. Week after week, I stayed on the public defender making sure he was working and questioning him on everything related to the case. I shared with him things I researched and anything to help my brother's case. I could tell he wasn't used to having someone knowledgeable like me hounding him. No, I wasn't an attorney, but I was his biggest advocate. I think I worked his nerves so much he gave me his personal cell number and was willing to meet me on a Saturday. Public defenders just don't usually do that. He thought by meeting we could get it all out and maybe I wouldn't bug him as much, but it wasn't likely. We eventually met and discussed the character statements and he was instructed to give it to the person over the state's attorney who tried to intimidate me.

Over a year later, a court date was set for sentencing. A couple of his church members came along with me and my mom. That time it was only us in the room. We sat on the front row and before I could sit down the state's attorney approached me. My heart wanted to drop. He asked if he could speak with me. Now that really made me nervous and all those with me had a bewildered expression on their face as they wondered what it was about. We proceeded to walk into the hallway, and he looked at me and said, "Never in all my years has this happened. My boss received all the character statements and your mom's letter and was touched. She agreed to offer your brother seven years minus the time he's served." I practically screamed knowing that God heard my cries. All the late nights, court dates, running back and forth, finding sitters for my children, high phone bills, and everything involved was not in vain. God heard my cries. He showed favor and mercy.

    As we entered back into the courtroom the judge read his sentence and we all celebrated outside the courtroom. God spared my brother's life. Before we left, the public defender thanked me and said how lucky my brother was to have me fighting for him. He said that I did all the work and that he wasn't needed. I just did what I thought was necessary to prevent from losing another brother.

    Another part in this chapter was over. Although I was happy his life was spared, it wasn't necessarily a win. It felt so out of place and weird celebrating knowing the details. How could we be so happy when sadly it still wouldn't bring my brother back? The joy, if I was able to find any, was that I had succeeded in not losing *another* brother.

Even though that part was over, it was on to the next phase. My brother was able to relax a little bit knowing that he had his sentence handed down and could prepare his mind for what was in front of him. It was just a matter of getting through it. He would have to serve four full years. It wasn't like I didn't think he wouldn't serve any time. I knew that even when we repent, we still must accept responsibility for our actions and eventually pay the cost of sin. He would have to serve his time but also live with his actions and the consequences.

Our brother was never coming back whether he served four or forty years. Trying to support him through that while serving time was just as difficult. Sometimes he would call and was upbeat as he could be. Other times he was depressed and scared. It was such a huge emotional rollercoaster for us both. I was completely worn out. As the natural encourager, at some point if I give and give without being replenished, I shut down but that was impossible with this situation. It was all God who gave me the strength because I was physically, mentally, and emotionally running on empty.

If it wasn't taking calls, I was writing him letters. Incarcerated people look for outside communication because it gets them through. It's an opportunity to connect with the outside world. There really wasn't a lot of outside support, if any, so everything pretty much fell in my lap. Everyone was still trying to get through what happened and people grieve and reach forgiveness at different points in their lives. It wasn't for me to judge them but to do what I was called to do and during this whole ordeal God called me to stand in the gap. It sure would have eased the burden some if I had had more family support. I mean my husband was there, but I couldn't expect him to take off work as frequently as I was running around regarding the case. He did what he could and supported me. After all, we still had a family and household to tend to. Someone had to be sane during this horrific situation. I just thank God I had his help.

Before sentencing, my brother was in the county jail, but once the sentence was handed down, they shipped him off to a town that was millions of miles away. At least he would finally become as settled as you mentally can in prison and train his mind to know he wouldn't be getting out for four years. It wouldn't be easy, and I'd have to factor in allotting at least eight hours when I could go visit him.

ROUND FOUR

Fighting for Family

Remember the Lord, who is great and awesome, and fight for your families...
—*Nehemiah 4:14 NIV*

Every part of this situation created different phases to get through but through it all God kept providing, protecting, and fueling me when I felt like it was overwhelming.

My brother had been laid to rest, the other brother sentenced and preparing to be transferred. I still had my third brother who was there and involved in the fight. He was extremely close with my deceased brother. They did everything together. I couldn't imagine what he must have been dealing with internally. I didn't know all the details of the altercation, but however it happened was and could be traumatic for anyone.

We started to gradually see him change after the tragedy and it was a slow painful process to watch. He was quieter, always looking over his shoulder and honestly, not the person we all knew. Oftentimes, he came over to my house and played the game with my youngest son. Other times he would come over and just sit very quietly. Anytime I would ask if he wanted to talk, his answer was always 'no.' If you asked him if he was okay, he would reply 'yes' but as a mom and living in the same tragedy as him, I knew that couldn't be true. I was still having a hard time dealing with it myself. I constantly wondered how it made him feel to see me support our other brother in jail, but he never said anything about it. He would ask about him here and there but there was no real conversation about it.

The weeks whizzed by and he just seemed to get worse. My husband even picked up on it. One day he sat down to have a talk with him. The conclusion was just that he was just having a hard time getting over it and that was understandable.

After a while everyone noticed the change in his behavior. At that point, I mentioned to my mom that he was really acting differently, and he needed some help. He started having weird conversations and asking questions that were odd. It even started to affect him at work, and he was fired. I didn't like the pattern I saw.

I'm not sure what happened, but one weekend he wound up in the mental hospital for a couple of days. My mom went to the hospital and spoke with his Nigerian doctor and was informed that he was fine, that he knew the word of God, and if he had a pastor my mom should get him in to see him. The doctor said he was going through something spiritual. He was having a hard time dealing with the loss. But what I didn't know that I found out by the incident was that he was on medication and apparently wasn't taking it.

Sadly, in the black community going to a psychiatrist or counselor isn't something that's proudly spoken well of. People assume you're crazy. There was no way any of us could have gone through this and not needed counseling.

Once they let him out, I tried to assure him that he could talk to me about anything whenever he wanted to in hopes of getting him to open up. Nothing worked. Some days he appeared to be his old self but then there were periods where I could sense that he was not okay. It was so much to deal with. Constantly worrying about my family, keeping communication open with my incarcerated brother, and watching my other brother appear to be on the verge of a mental breakdown was all a bit much. It was so obvious that he was struggling internally.

My hands were full, and I just didn't know what else to do. I kept leaning on God and my family to get the strength to keep pushing and trying to be what everyone else needed me to be. I tried my hardest to hold myself together. It was not easy, and I felt like a yoyo being pulled in so many directions, praying I wouldn't break.

Time went on and the years started to pass. Life never stops. We keep moving. My husband had driven me four hours one way to see my incarcerated brother numerous times and I hated going there. I wanted to see him in person to make sure he was okay, but the place made me cringe. It wasn't the nicest, most positive atmosphere to be going in. He was taken to Menard Correctional Facility to serve his time which is known for being one of the most dangerous prisons. They were rude and I honestly hated all the searching and formalities you had to go through just for a thirty-minute visit where they really didn't want you hugging.

We sat at a table with all eyes on us with occasional warnings of not being allowed to do this or that. But we made the best of it. For those thirty minutes he was able to get out of his cell and have a conversation for a few moments. My husband is a jokester and always found a way to get him to laugh and that made me happy. Those thirty minutes went by so fast and I was always saddened to leave but happy to have the chance to see him in person.

During his calls I could always tell when he was having a bad day or going through something, but he never told me for not wanting me to worry. I couldn't imagine the survival skills you would need to make it in prison but all I could do was say my see you laters, accept the calls, write the letters and make sure he had money for his commissary.

Life continued to happen, and my other brother continued to show signs of mental illness. It was heartbreaking to watch. The years were passing for our incarcerated brother to get out of jail and it seemed like he was getting worse. I wondered how it would be with him out and how my other brother would feel. Between the two of them and God, they were the only ones who really knew what happened. There were three of them in the altercation and one was no longer here to tell his side of the story. *How will they be finally facing each other again?*

The time neared for his release, and the incarcerated brother went before the prison review board. To be released he had to have an address and the only place he could come was to my house. Once again, I found myself in another phase of this unbearable process. That meant that a parole officer would have to show up frequently at my house armed with protective gear to see him. This made me wonder how my neighbors would look at us. Some of our neighbors were not so nice and I personally didn't like the whole idea of the parole officer showing up like that, but it was for his own protection. It didn't matter that my brother wasn't some mass killer; they didn't know or care about that. They just had a job to do. I knew it was for the officers' safety, but I just didn't like the appearance of it. But I was his only option.

The day came and my brother was finally released. They gave him a few dollars to get the bus and my husband and I met him at the 95th Street bus station late that night. We pulled up and there he was, getting off the bus with a box of his belongings he had while serving time. It was overflowing with hundreds of letters and cards I sent him to keep him encouraged.

It was so strange to watch him just walking around my house and looking almost as if he was still locked up. My husband mentioned that it would take some time for him to get back used to having his freedom. I showed him his room and laid down for the night but couldn't help wondering what was next. This whole traumatic experience had constantly been a matter of going through the stages to prepare for the next and it was emotionally and physically draining.

Morning came and after breakfast he prepared for a visit with the probation officer. No lies, I wasn't looking forward to that part and when he arrived, I knew why. An officer pulled right up in front of my elderly neighbors' home. We are talking about a couple who nurtured their grass so much that they complained if a ball rolled in their yard. So, imagine seeing a probation officer getting out of the car in an affluent neighborhood with his bullet proof vest and guns approaching my house. I think I had the nosiest neighbors of all time.

I walked toward the door as I saw him walking toward the house because I wanted to get it over with as soon as possible. I'd be lying if I said I didn't have an attitude about him having come to my house. I don't know if I thought maybe my brother would be ordered to go check in somewhere. Heck, I hadn't ever experienced any of this. Anyone who knows me knows I talk with my face so you could only imagine the look I had. He introduced himself and I called my brother down. While we waited in the foyer, I just let it out. I asked him if he really had to show up armed like that.

"My brother isn't a hardened criminal and I know what you must deal with day to day, but this won't be like any of those cases. He made a mistake and it was our brother." The officer explained that it was protocol and for his own safety. I understood that but I think it was just a lot of built up emotions and I was just tired all around. I didn't want any issues with the subdivision I lived in. I didn't like the appearance of it.

As he did a drop for my brother, he explained how the process would go. He would show up scheduled and/or unannounced. Each time he would have to have his urine checked and remain clean. He explained to my brother how lucky and blessed he was to come out to these living arrangements and that a lot of the released men don't have places to stay. He was given instructions on job training and resources. *So, that's the next step.*

I planned a day off work so that I could drive him to the office. There were so many people everywhere and the workers weren't friendly at all. The lines were long, and we wound up being there for hours. After a while, my brother started to complain and asked if he had to wait in the long lines because he wasn't going to do it. That frustrated me. I had taken off work to help him and we both were waiting so that really rubbed me the wrong way, especially when he decided he wasn't doing it. I lost it and told him how I felt. When we got home, I headed to my bedroom to lie down. That's when I heard him slam the door. So, I went downstairs and asked what the problem was and told him that I wasn't going to deal with his attitude and erratic behavior after all I tried to do for him.

I knew he was frustrated but I was at the end of my rope and couldn't handle any more, so I informed him that I thought it would be best that he found somewhere else to stay. It broke my heart, but I'd run myself in the ground and doing it alone, outside of my husband, was a lot for me. I wasn't abandoning him because I was the only support system he had, but I just couldn't keep going like that. I was done being all in. I needed to help from a distance.

The weekend came and he had asked for a ride to the train. I dropped him off and gave him some money and explained that I'd be there to support as much as I could, but I really needed him to get himself together. Even though I did as much as possible to help him, he still needed to do things to help himself. That would be the best 'thank you' he could give me and the only payback I expected of him.

We all found ourselves in a situation that would demand something so different from each of us to be able to get through and handle all that came with it. Our sweet brother Lorenzo had passed, and our family would never be the same again. I had to do all I could to somehow try and find some ray of light in such a dark place. None of us could have ever imagined going through this and somehow God was going to get the glory from this tragedy. He had to.

The devil couldn't and wouldn't win this fight. Lorenzo couldn't die in vain. I didn't know how it would all look at the end. One thing I knew for sure was that God used me to be light for whatever reason, whether I thought I could handle it or not. I didn't have a choice in the matter and from day one my heart was steered toward trying to do the right thing in an unfathomable situation. No one ever asks to walk in situations like this. I'm sure if my brothers could go back this would have never happened. Because I knew that in my heart, I had to move in a way that I had never in my entire life.

You never know how strong you are until you face something that requires you to dig deeper than you ever have. Until you're forced to reach deep down into a place that requires you to operate out of yourself where you know that the only way you can muster up the strength is if God gives it to you. A place where you recognize the experience for what it is but to move through it you must press harder and without total understanding of the steps, the why or even the how.

Some time went on and things started to get back to somewhat normal. My brother would come visit here and there and we communicated over the phone. One weekend he came up for a visit. My other brother who was involved came over with a cousin and they all were going out. I couldn't help but wonder how they both felt seeing each other for the first time. It appeared to be okay but sometimes we can hide things well. They came back after the evening and everything seemed fine. I didn't ask any questions. Honestly, I didn't know how or what to say, or if I should say anything at all.

A couple of weeks went by and my brother who had been dealing with some of the beginning stages of mental illness spent a lot of time at my house. He moved about ten minutes from me, and I saw him often. I couldn't help but notice how something really seemed off with him. He was really struggling with our brother's death and it seemed like it had gotten worse once our other brother was released. I talked to him many times about going to get some help, but he always refused. I'd explained to him that going through this was hard enough for me and I wasn't there and that it had to be even harder with him witnessing our brother dying.

Things got progressively worse. He moved in with my mom and her boyfriend. They didn't live too far from me, so I still saw him often. Occasionally, my mom complained about how he was acting, and I saw it myself. It didn't stop me from always trying to talk to him and do a wellness check-in, but he continued to decline going to counseling. I even had my husband talk to him about it with no luck.

I continued to fight to be the light in the family and support and help when and where I could. I finally moved on to pursuing schooling in health and fitness. It was something that I had slacked on and when I finally made time for me and saw changes, it motivated me to become certified. Amidst everything I'd been through and continued to go through, Tasha was carving out time for Tasha. *Finally.*

I rode the train every morning to downtown Chicago for class four days a week. One morning my husband and I were getting dressed to leave the house and the news was on. There was a story my husband had been watching about a shooting of a man who lived in a nearby neighborhood who was killed by SWAT. I didn't pay attention to the details. I only tuned in here and there.

We all left the house and continued with our day. My husband was at work and I was in class. There was always a lunch break around one and that was when I had an opportunity to go to the lockers and check my phone. I had missed a lot of calls and the one I returned was from our youngest brother.

"Tasha, I'm really sorry to have to tell you this, but Brandon was shot and killed this morning." I was in the locker room screaming to the top of my lungs when another classmate ran to grab the instructor. All I remember was her holding me and walking me out to go home for the day. Apparently, my husband had already notified the school and was on his way to get to me before anyone could reach me. So, once I got to the car, he was a bit upset that someone had called to tell me knowing that I was in school.

As we drove home, I was totally out of it and so confused. Once again, I was dealing with losing a brother violently. Two younger brothers, both in their twenties were gone. You read or see this on TV, but never would you think it could happen to you or your family. *Why would someone shoot my brother?* I didn't know any details so all I could do was try and process hearing the news in my mind, but my husband asked me if I remembered the news story of a shooting that morning. *Somewhat.* Truthfully, I really hadn't been paying the news much attention. He informed me that the story was about my brother. Details were still coming out, but he had been killed by SWAT. I was devastated.

We were told earlier that day that there had been a man on the southside wearing a long trench coat on a hot 90's summer day and someone called the police reporting that he was armed. From what I was told, when the officers approached him they claimed that he shot at one officer's foot and ran. Witnesses say he barricaded himself in between two apartment buildings and they recall the shootout with police lasting from 10:30 pm until 12:30 am. Countless shots were fired back and forth hours into the night. People in the neighborhood described how disturbing it was hearing the exchange of gunfire back and forth until SWAT was called.

Chicago police called SWAT and they had a helicopter flying over the buildings he supposedly was barricaded between. Neighbors reported that the shooting went on for hours and that they couldn't sleep. Other than the scenes from movies I watched, I knew nothing of SWAT. On the screen, SWAT would often call family members to convince them to surrender and to my knowledge they hadn't called us at all. *How could this be that my brother was involved and why didn't anyone call a family member to try and talk him out if this was actually the case?* Maybe we could have gotten through to him.

Death is already hard enough but when a loved one dies a violent death, it's an unimaginable process to experience. My head was spinning while visualizing my brother being shot up multiple times by a slew of police.

The night before this horrific ordeal, there were reports that a man killed an officer and was still on the run, so the police were probably hot-headed and on alert. When they approached my brother. not knowing he was somewhat mentally ill, he probably panicked and got scared. There were also reports that the person they had been looking for was a dark-skinned man and clearly my brother was high yellow. I guess the officers were not trained on how to approach and deal with mentally ill people. If you see someone in August and it's ninety degrees outside, it will appear that something is definitely wrong.

The story was something I couldn't even believe. They wanted to convince me that Brandon was shooting at the police. *But why?* He was never a violent person. To my knowledge, he wasn't in the streets, nor did he get into any trouble. *Were they even sure it was him doing the shooting? How could he have gotten in a situation like this? I need more answers. I can't wrap my mind around this at all. This is not the Brandon that I knew. Had his level of mental illness gotten worse than any of us imagined? Did we miss the extent of his illness and just didn't know who he was anymore?*

I couldn't believe that about him. If it were true and he was shooting, he was not in his right frame of mind. The death of our brother had really taken a toll on him and he was silently suffering inside. My brother had fallen mentally ill from not dealing with the trauma of his best friend's death. Being there watching our brother take his last breath after saying that he didn't want to die had broken everything inside of Brandon.

All those years he suffered silently. He indeed changed. We often noticed him more paranoid and sometimes the conversations were confusing but other times he seemed like his normal self. I don't think anyone can go through something as traumatizing as this was for him, for all of us, and not change. After his mental hospital stay, I learned for the first time that he had in fact been put on medication and wasn't taking it. If I had known that it had gone that far, I definitely would have pressed harder for him to seek help on a continuous basis. He never wanted to go for fear of someone thinking he was crazy.

I didn't know whether to be angry or hurt more. I needed someone to give me answers. A SWAT team had brutally killed my brother firing multiple shots causing him to suffer a painful death. I couldn't help but think of how alone, confused and scared he was as multiple SWAT officers fired at him. *He was ill and they didn't have to shoot him like that. Couldn't they see he wasn't okay when they approached him? Why couldn't two officers just handcuff him and take him to the station? Maybe they would have seen that he needed help.*

I found myself rehearsing in my mind how he died and reading the article from the shooting multiple times. Seeing images of the bullet shells marked in a gangway knowing that those bullets were lodged in my brother's body made my soul cringe. Those visuals confirmed that he really suffered and must have bled to death.

I couldn't stop crying and repeatedly replaying the scenario over in my mind. I was astounded that the story we saw on the news was a story of my brother being killed. Even though I hadn't paid it much attention, I knew that the person had died and to find out it was my brother was painful. Unable to make the thoughts stop, I knew I would have to face my mom again as she grieved another young son under the age of 25 dying a tragic death. As my husband drove me to her house, I couldn't even find the words to say that would give her any comfort. We had been down this road before just with different circumstances. The thought that SWAT killed him like they did was totally unbearable.

It was even more disturbing when I arrived at her house and she told me about a scary situation she woke up to. Brandon had been staying with my mom. When she woke, she smelled gas and got up to check it out, but when she attempted to open the door, she was unable to. Brandon had tied a string to her door to prevent her from getting out. She woke her boyfriend up and he forcefully pulled the door open to find that my brother tied the string from her door to another door in the house. They discovered all the eyes on the stove were on just enough to give off gas.

Dear God, this mental illness was way bigger than any of us had ever thought. Was he trying to get her attention? Was he angry at her? Or was his illness expressing his deep pain toward my mom. She said she had been calling him all that day, but no answer. That was the first that I learned of the situation. We could have alerted police to look for him and clue them in on what was going on. Maybe they would have approached him differently instead of becoming trigger happy.

All the signs were apparent of severe mental illness. He had really struggled with losing his best friend, our brother. Being there to watch him take his last breath and utter how he didn't want to die had caused my brother to lose his mind. All my talks with him begging and pleading when he came over to my house had failed. My husband had even tried getting through to him but to no avail. I sat there as reality set in. We were facing another tragedy, another loss and having to bury another brother under the age of 25. *My God.*

For the second time, my husband and I had to go through the familiar process of making arrangements because he too had no insurance. It was a very painful situation to be in again but as with my other brother, we got it all done.

The day before the service, my husband drove me to the funeral home and I just couldn't believe I was burying another younger brother.

As I walked up to the casket and saw him lying there, I felt speechless and empty inside. Watching him lifeless in a casket having faced a tragic death was more than a notion. I wasn't sure what condition we'd find him in. We knew that he had been shot multiple times so my husband was curious and touched him to see that it appeared he had been wrapped before they had gotten him together. I was crushed.

The service was the next day and a much smaller one than our other brother had. He was somewhat of a loner as well and it was being held at the actual funeral home. We did what we could and sat through service finding ourselves broken and distraught that we had to face this again. That time was different only because my brother who had served time was attending. As I sat through the service weak and mentally exhausted, I wondered how he would feel once we arrived at the cemetery and saw that the other brother had been buried there as well. We were just steps away.

When I chose Lorenzo's headstone, I picked one with his picture etched into it. So, there I was sitting through one brother's service wanting to shelter the last living brother from any more hurt. Doing so, I felt like I was hurting myself because I just didn't have it in me to handle any more breakdowns. *Not today.* Knowing that he may see Lorenzo's picture nearby, I texted family members and requested that they not inform him that Brandon's plot was so close to Lorenzo's. *Please just not today.* He could come back another day and make peace. It was all too much for me and I needed to avoid any extra layers as much as possible.

It was extremely heartbreaking for me. Not only did I lose two younger brothers, but I lost both to violent deaths and I was headed to the cemetery where they would be buried a few feet away from each other. I can't even explain how traumatizing it was for me mentally. *Years ago, when I stood at this exact cemetery selecting a plot for our other brother, I never would have never imagined that I'd now find myself standing here again burying another brother practically side by side.*

It hurt me so badly and I really wanted God to fill me in on what exactly He was doing because I didn't understand it. I needed to know why we had to experience something so traumatic to this degree. After going through both of those deaths, I became more hurt and angrier by the days. I couldn't wrap my mind around it or understand it. I was not necessarily mad at God, but angry that the enemy had stormed through our family and ripped our entire hearts out and left us fighting the memories surrounding their untimely deaths. He found an entryway and took advantage forcing us to live our lives without them.

They were best friends. When you saw one, you saw the other. They attended school together, worked together and now they are lying dead and buried at the cemetery together. *Things like this just don't happen, at least not to us.* That's how it felt. I've heard of sad stories like this but now I was forced to live this new tragic reality and it was devastating. It did happen to us and we were left rehearsing the details of what happened to our dear loved ones. We never thought something like this could happen to our family. Up until today, when I think about it, I still can't believe it.

We arrived at the cemetery and as the minister prayed and laid my brother to rest, I saw a family member who knew that Lorenzo was buried there drawing attention to his grave site. Eventually, what I tried to prevent from happening is precisely what happened.

My brother made his way over to where they were all standing, and I just didn't know how to react. I couldn't help but wonder how he truly felt. He didn't attend his funeral service for obvious reasons and I'm sure he had asked God for forgiveness. But to be standing six feet above where his younger brother lay surely surfaced so many emotions. It definitely brought them up for me. Meanwhile, we were already dealing with another tragic loss. Watching him for the first time standing above our brother's grave after just burying another one just minutes and steps away made me so sad. I just wished I could make it go away. That was a burden he would carry the rest of his life. No one would ever know how he felt or what our siblings went through. Lorenzo's death was a lot to process and it seemed Brandon had struggled internally denying help for too long. This was a lot for any of us to deal with, but I couldn't help wondering what my brother was experiencing as he stood there.

There's no one on this earth that could have ever told me that something on this level would come and attack our world. An even greater sadness arose over my body because, after all, I was the big sister and I never wanted to see any of them hurt. I wanted to fix things and protect them, but that was another time it was totally out of my control. All I was forced to do was go through these horrible events along with them. The fact is that as much as I wanted to, I couldn't prevent any of us from going through things, so I did my best to be there for them. I tried to step in where I could.

This family was hurt and in turmoil. The enemy had just come and wreaked havoc on my family and I had no choice but to lean on and trust God. The weight of it all was so heavy. My mom lost two young sons tragically and had one serve time for the death. It was just unfathomable. As a mom, I couldn't even begin to know what she was experiencing.

There we all stood in the cemetery lost, hurt, confused, and wounded. Our family chain had been broken forever, not once but twice amongst siblings. We departed the cemetery leaving two people who were and always be a part of our lives. Two people who walked through life together are now buried together. We left with feelings that none of us could explain even with the best try. Each one of us grieving in very different ways. Pieces of our hearts were broken and only God could mend. How would we go on after such traumatic deaths? We experienced tremendous losses that were our new reality. Those voids would always be there. It was too much for one family to ever endure and one we would never wish on another family.

*****

There were no discussions in the family about the tragedy surrounding my brothers. We didn't say more than we had to discuss. None of us wanted to make the other feel any more pain than we already felt. It wasn't discussed amongst us or anyone else. Why would I want to go around sharing something so painful? The only thing I wanted to do was to protect the hearts of all involved from my mom to my siblings. I never even had it in me to talk to my brother whom I fought for to find out what happened that caused them to fight and lead to this horrible incident of our brother dying and him serving time for it. He had enough reminders and things to face and, in my mind, bringing it up would only cause added pain for him.

After my brother was killed by SWAT and I returned to class, I couldn't even begin to bring myself to share with anyone how he died and hoped no one would dare to ask me. The program director did ask and all I could say was that he was shot. I couldn't speak of the circumstances surrounding it. It was on the news and in the paper, and after his death I logged on numerous times to read the articles repeatedly still not believing something like that could have happened to someone in my own family.

I Googled my brother's name numerous times day in and day out. I listened to the witnesses in the neighborhood that spoke of not being able to sleep through the night because of the countless shots being fired. I carried a feeling in my chest that made me cringe with sheer pain that was so unbearable. I imagined it so many ways that it overwhelmed me. It took some time before I could bring myself to stop Googling the story.

It was gut-wrenching and although I was going through it, reading articles, and listening to the few interviews, my mind and heart still wouldn't allow me to accept or process any of it. No matter how many times I fought within myself to stop reading the articles, I kept going to them. In some way, I thought that maybe I would read or hear something different and figure out what really happened. Sadly, nothing helped to make me believe it was a reality.

I would constantly imagine how scared he must have felt there all alone barricaded in between buildings trying to decide how to get himself out of a tough situation. *Was he even in a good place mentally to even think that far?* The fear and pain he must have felt with nowhere to run or the pain he must have felt with each bullet entering his body. Shot after shot. I imagined it all. The pain, the bleeding, the fall with each bullet. I wondered where he was shot, and which bullet took his last breath. That was my brother and I couldn't wrap my mind around any of it. It hurt in ways I can never explain to this day. I still get the thoughts. Things still trigger my wonder.

These are all the things that continuously played in my mind. The struggle mentally within myself rehearsing what I thought the scene may have looked. I saw it on TV many times before. Numerous cars of police with firearms drawn just firing shots. Well, this time it wasn't a TV show and it wasn't an actor. It was real life and it was one of my younger brothers.

My sister and I struggled wondering if we could handle reading the police report or obtaining the autopsy. After going back and forth, we decided against it. My heart just couldn't take it. We knew the suffering he must have endured but seeing and reading it would only overwhelm us more. That was something we did not need to have embedded in our memories of our brother.

Sometimes, even after all these years, I question if I'm in a better place and can request the report because no one truly knows what happened besides being killed by a Chicago SWAT Team. Just recently the subject came up with my sister and she mentioned a family member describing how his clothes were still bloody when they picked them up. Years later, I know I couldn't handle it and as hard as it is, I don't want to remember him that way. I still can't watch any movie or show that involves SWAT because of the triggers. Those scenes are still hard for me to handle.

When I lost my grandmother, seeing kids with their grandparents brought back memories of how close we were. Sometimes I just stare longing to have those moments with her again. I remember once I had to take my son for an outpatient test at the hospital and as we waited, I saw an older lady waiting for her test that looked so much like my grandmother that it was almost scary. She had the same hair color and sweet demeanor. Even my son thought so too, so I wasn't just imagining things. Triggers are a real thing and you need strategies on how to work through them.

Those of us who know trauma also know that you can't control the triggers or when they happen. Many of us don't have the coping tools to be able to handle them when they happen. Maybe, like me, you just bury the feelings and float through life barely dealing with the hurt, avoiding anything that resembles what you went through. Maybe you bury it all in the back of your mind in hopes that the details of the tragedies will just go away. They may go away for the time being but they're always there. Life won't get better until you actively and intentionally deal with those thoughts and emotions.

ROUND FIVE

Fighting to Write

Your story could be the key that unlocks someone else's prison. Don't be afraid to share it.
—Unknown

Now begins the moment of my transparency to you. I realize this book may not be for everyone, but what I do know is that I spent many years fighting writing this book. Just thinking of writing gave me anxiety. Yet, I received numerous prophetic words over my life regarding this book. There was surely a strong fight to get here and that is the reason that I had to write this book. You see, the enemy thought he could take me through all these things to break me, destroy my future and hinder me in reaching those I'm called to. His plan was to stop me from fulfilling my God given purpose in this life.

While I endured the pain of my circumstances, I felt weak and defeated. I constantly questioned, why me? *Why not me?* No, I didn't want my loved ones to experience such tragic deaths. I would never have wanted my brother to serve time for our brother's death or have the other one murdered by SWAT. If I had my way, my family would have never gone through any of this. My siblings wouldn't have had to process the pain of losing siblings. No, I wouldn't have wanted my mom to have experienced the loss of two of her young sons. No way would I have ever wanted to sit at the bedside of my grandmother for six long months for her to pass away leaving me feeling lost without her. But through it all, God carried me.

He carried me through some of the most heartbreaking moments in my life and although I felt like each time I couldn't make it through, God equipped me with a strength that only He could provide. Any one of these things could have taken me out or caused me to mentally break down. Any one of these deaths could have made me look for other avenues to cope that were out of character for me but the grace of God stepped in and put a force and love so great within me that I was able to keep pushing forward. For that reason, I know that if this book reaches and touches one person who has gone through the pain of trauma or is currently experiencing it, He kept me just for you. He ordained this moment specifically for you, and though I feel I may be late in writing it, I'm right on time for you!

My pain and struggles never caused me to question my faith. If anything, they made it stronger because now I see that even amid trauma, God was preparing me for you. He was preparing the hands of a ready writer who would heal and deliver those who needed me in this hour. Everything in life we face is not by accident. We may not see or understand it at the time, but He always reveals Himself. God would not take me through a pain so deep as the pain I felt not to turn it around to use it for my good. That's why I had to fight was so hard to write. That's why as I wrote this book, I suffered severe headaches and palpitations sometimes.

The enemy was defeated the moment I began to muster up the strength to type every word of this book because in my weakness God made me strong. I got up enough courage to finally do it so I could share my experience with you. He allowed me this moment just for you and for me to see that my family didn't die in vain. If I'm able to touch just one person and that one person is you, then I have done my job. If I'm blessed to reach more, praise God! However, if I fought the good fight and overcame this struggle for you who may be at your wit's end, suffering in silence and still struggling with trauma, I am okay with that. If you don't know if you can or will make it, this book was written just for you and you were worth the struggle it took for me to open and pour my heart out to you. You were worth fighting for! The late nights and early mornings were not in vain. You were worth reliving the trauma. God graced me to write this book for you.

From the start of this book until now, I've shared my personal stories with you. Tragedies that I never opened up about were spread before you. When I say I understand what you're going through, it's coming from a place of personal experiences. When I say I understand how you feel it's because I do and it's not out of routine. I've fought the pain. I've silently cried myself to sleep at night. I've experienced every emotion under the sun. I've felt hopeless, alone and scared about what going through all these tragedies did to me internally.

In a feeble attempt to suppress the hurt, I masked the pain that I felt. I didn't or couldn't talk about it. Maybe I wanted to talk, but never felt strong enough to speak on it. I refused to share parts of this story with anyone. It was just too painful to relive.

As you were reading this book, I believe that you too may have suffered tragedy and loss and could connect with some of my feelings. Maybe you didn't experience exactly what I went through, but you have your own story. If not, perhaps you're aware of people and families who have experienced loss on this level. You saw this book and it spoke to your spirit or it resonated with you for whatever reason.

    I don't believe you picked this book up by chance, accident or because the cover grabbed your attention. If you've experienced tragedy some parts of my story opened up new and old wounds, made you uncomfortable, made tears well up in your eyes, forced you to feel feelings you've avoided, relived your own personal experiences and made you want to close the book. You may have even decided that you aren't ready to address your past or current trauma. Maybe not. Just maybe it opened your eyes to see that you're not as healed as you thought you were. You are still hurt, angry and recognized that you never healed properly. You too suppressed the trauma or felt ashamed of what you went through. Your weakness made it difficult to talk about it or seek help.

    If you haven't personally experienced trauma, maybe this book opened your insight to what people go through quietly while still moving through life appearing unbothered. Now you understand how people can find a way to function day in and day out going unnoticed while harboring deep pain. People you see every day are fighting inner turmoil. You now get how we can walk around and look okay on the outside but are a mess inside. Many are fighting battles nobody knows about.

Did it touch your heart in a way that you'll judge less when you see that person who may be quiet and reserved? That kid, woman, man, boy or girl acting out may be viewed as weird, troublesome, and be labeled as thinking they're better than others because they don't talk or fit in. If you look hard enough and take time to notice, you'll find the reason for all these things.

Maybe you developed a new level of compassion for your brother or sister whom you fellowship with every Sunday in church or work. Just maybe, my heartfelt cries triggered something in you to see people and life's experiences with a different lens. Begin to pay attention to those around you who need your help and intervene when safe to do so with a heart of compassion. You see we are all fighting something.

If you've found yourself on the side of having gone through traumatic events, I pray you will begin to do the inner work needed to heal and find closure in your life and move on to become all that God called you to be--happy, healthy and whole. Take a real hard look inside and examine the parts of your heart that continue to hurt, keep you up at night or keep you from moving forward. Address those memories and flashbacks caused by going through traumatic events. The night terrors, the blame game, the what if I did this, the what if I did that, the guilt, the shame, the feeling less than, the unworthiness, the not measuring up or the lacking confidence. Whatever it is. Your story will be different than mine, but all our stories can have a beautiful ending if we allow God to heal us and gather the courage to do the work.

Maybe you're questioning why and how a loving God would allow you to experience so much pain. You were left wondering what you did to deserve it. *Am I loved or capable of being loved after all I've gone through?* You have been torn down by the circumstances of life that were completely out of your human control. You are still not able to see what life looks like on the other side of this.

It does not matter whether the pain you experienced was a result of life just happening or by the hands of another or even self-inflicted. Perhaps you were hurt by the tragic events you were forced to face or things that you didn't ask to face. You have mentally, physically, and emotionally relinquished your power to the thing, circumstance or the people who hurt you. No human or circumstance is worth it. It's time to learn how to do the work.

We have false senses of coping mechanisms that are not long-lasting, so we move through life like a hamster on a wheel just going in circles with no real destination. We follow other people's timeline in the grieving process to just get by. Meanwhile, we are not acknowledging what we went through or realizing that we need to stop and make sure we are okay. To get to our healing, it will take looking at the parts that seem to lead us to unsafe and unrealistic ways to maneuver through life. We must truly deal with the stuff that we choose to bury inside because it hurts too much.

We must release the pain and damage caused by what people did or said to us. Their lack of understanding the process it takes to recover and heal from trauma may have prompted them to speak out of their ignorance. People impose their opinions on us as it relates to what they would do in a situation or how we should be. It's okay not to be okay. It's okay to acknowledge how you feel. It's okay to be hurt, grieve and all the other feelings we go through; it's just not okay to stay there.

You have a right to be angry, cry and feel all the emotions that come with the pain you may be feeling right now, have felt in the past or will feel in the future. I've been there and felt each of these emotions and fought to push through, sometimes only to find myself stuck. I ended up hurt all over again, angry, mad, disgusted, just an emotional wreck. My insides were crying but I ignored my feelings. At times, it was all for the sake of not wanting to deal with the trauma of what the experience or pain made me feel.

Let me tell you right now that your feelings are valid, and you have a right to heal in your own time and not the time someone else dictates. If you've experienced trauma, no one can tell you how long to grieve or minimize your personal experience with dealing with what you faced. Acknowledge for yourself what the trauma caused you. Acknowledge how it made you feel. Acknowledge what you're feeling right now, what you're experiencing and the struggle you're in to push past it. Your feelings are valid. Your feelings are valid. Your feelings are valid. Repeat it three times or as many times as it takes for you to believe it for yourself. *My feelings are valid.*

From this day forward, don't suppress your internal feelings ever again. Don't ignore the areas that this book hit. I am referring to those deep and unknown feelings that only you and God are aware of. He can help you and you're not alone. Again, I say your feelings matter and you have a right to feel and not feel guilty about the fights that you have fought. Don't close this book without acknowledging those pieces of you that still need healing. Those pieces that still silently cry out for help need to be made whole.

There were so many layers of hurt and pain that I'm just now starting to work through years later. Don't let that be you. And if you have waited years to begin your healing process, don't be ashamed. If you're living, it's not too late. You must get it out. Why? Because your future is worth the fight to come back whole and stronger than what you went through. It's bigger than what the tragedy did to you. It's mightier than who caused the trauma or the people who mishandled you. It's even more powerful than what you may have done to yourself.

Life happens to us all and is often out of our control. Could I control my brothers dying? *No.* Could I control the circumstances surrounding their deaths? *No.* Could I control determining whether my brother served anytime at all? *No.* Could I control being abused as a young girl by my mom's husband and watching him go from each child to my mom? *No.* Could I control my grandma dying? *No.* Could I control pain others caused me up until now or will in the future? *No.* Can I look for ways to guard myself? *Yes.* Can I have measures in place to handle the challenges that I'll face in the future? *Yes.*

Each of the terrible experiences I've faced in my life were out of my control. There was nothing I did to deserve them happening. I didn't have the power to bring my loved ones back. I didn't have the power over the actions of people in my life who hurt me. Neither was I able to control how life hurt me by losing parts of my family. However, I have learned that I can control how I allow myself to move forward. I have control over my feelings and how much I allow God to heal my inner wounds so that I can become the woman and voice God can and will use to heal those I'm divinely called to. He allowed me to get to a place where I could reach back for you and that's the reason for this book.

    It's our responsibility to heal and take our power back from everything and everyone in our past. It doesn't mean it won't hurt or you'll forget it. It means there's no time like the present to begin the steps to start the process and let them, it, and the circumstances go. All of it. Cast them one by one at the feet of God so that He can make everything new and beautiful in His time. If God took you through it and brought you through it, then He has a reason and in due time you'll see why. I found my why and now it's time for you to take the steps to find yours.

    It's by the grace of God that I made it. I've worked on some things and am still working on others. I want you to begin the work too. If you're reading this and are still here, there's a great reason. God has His hands on you and He's waiting for you to tell Him just where it hurts. Give it to Him. There are still ways God wants to use you as well as what you faced, but it starts with you first.

The things you have experienced probably did not feel great while going through them but I can bet that after you are healed you'll see how He will begin to use your story like I'm using my story in hopes to help heal someone else. I didn't think I could ever share my heart and definitely not for the world to hear. If I hadn't started counseling and really braved the nerve to face my fears, I would not be sharing today.

    Multiple people who didn't know each other on various occasions said write the book. Years later, I found the courage to urge and inspire you to heal, process and begin to become that beautiful person God wants to use. As painful as it was going through, you'll live to share your story when the time is right. It may not be through a book, but whatever way God chooses will be great and impactful. At the right time and place.

    The only way I'm here to share my story is because God gave me the strength to make it through to the other side and I made up my mind that it was time to unmask the hurt and pain so that I could blossom. I became a part of a church that teaches deliverance and healing. I read books and took many self-development courses just to get here and I am still working.

So today, right now--not tomorrow or next week, but today--acknowledge where you presently are and commit to do the work. The world is waiting on you like it was waiting on me. Imagine all the people who were and are waiting on me that are called to me and the years it took to get here. Well, here I am years later sharing the things I thought would destroy me. Are you ready?

Below I want you to think about and list the areas that trigger you, cause pain, and areas where you still could use help.

_____

_____

_____

_____

_____

_____

_____

_____

Acknowledge what happened to you or the things you're struggling with.

I acknowledge:

_____

_____

_____

_____

_____

_____

_____

_____

_____

_____

_____

_____

_____

_____

_____

I confess out loud that I am not the circumstances or things that life threw at me. The people that hurt me, I give to God. It was not my fault. I release the guilt and shame. I acknowledge any areas of pain I'm feeling and recognize that I need help. Today, I choose to begin again. I will begin working to live my life to the fullest. Today, I begin to work on myself, take care of me and learn the tools it takes to move beyond my past. I choose to do it for me because I'm worth it. I'm a fighter and in a fight for my future. The other side of this is brighter and I'm stronger because of it.

Signature promise to self

X_____

Prayer Of Healing

Father God,

We submit everything that we are facing or have faced in the past. We acknowledge the things that happened and our feelings. Today, Lord, we take the necessary steps to begin our healing process. We let go and release so that you may step in and take total control. We know that nothing we have experienced caught You by surprise. Even during the times when we may have felt alone, You were right here carrying us through. You waited on us to give all our cares to you. You've seen every tear, every heartbreak and all the circumstances that caused us to become stagnant. You know the pain and grief that happened in our lives. But today, Father, we say we trust You. We love You and know that healing can and is ours as we submit our prayers and requests to You. We know that nothing is too hard for You. Psalms 56:8 says, You keep a track record of all our sorrows. You have collected all our tears in a bottle so that You may heal and comfort us. We humbly bow to You in surrenderance with arms outstretched wide crying, "Lord, we need You." We need You to touch those areas of our hearts that have become hardened. We need You to touch the secret place where only You can get through. Only You can feel and heal the voids we feel. Only You can reveal the plans You have for us and the ways You want to use our stories to strengthen and to heal others. Today, we say that we are ready to begin again, Lord. Father, we repent for not trusting You as we should have along the way, but today we say let the weight begin to fall off now. The weight of suppressing our feelings and putting up a wall to anything and anyone who tried to get through to us. We surrender it all. We ask You to guide us along the path to complete healing and restoration and we look forward to Your revelation of our experiences. For we know that there is always a reason for everything that happens in our lives. Reveal it to us. Father, thank You for carrying us and we praise You in advance for our complete and total healing.

Amen!

ROUND SIX

Fighting Through Trauma

There are wounds that never show on the body that are deeper and more hurtful than anything that bleeds.
—Laurel K. Hamilton

Trauma is defined by the American Psychological Association as the emotional response to an extremely negative event. While trauma is a normal reaction to overwhelming and tragic events in life, some of them can become severe enough that it begins to interfere in our day to day operations and how we move through life. Trauma can change how we view life and the lens we see things through.

When a person goes through trauma it activates the physiological responses that then alter neurological function. The event can then trigger responses within your body and most often those are negative responses. Cognitive functions can become affected by changes within your brain and then as a domino effect cause severe mental, physical, and emotional stress. You find yourself always in a flight or fight mode.

Flight or fight is the combination of different reactions to various types of stress. It's a survival mechanism. The symptomatic system sends out different impulses and the brain tells the adrenal glands to release a hormone called norepinephrine into the bloodstream. What's known as a stress hormone causes the body to react, sending the body into various changes, including, and not limited to, rises in blood pressure and increased heart rate.

Trauma can be caused by something so negative and overwhelming that it has an impact on not only your emotional well-being but mental stability, physical well-being as well as your spiritual health. Unchecked and unhealed trauma has caused families to walk around operating in cycles of dysfunction. Dysfunction is in the home, schools, and churches. Growing kids to adults are carrying those dysfunctions into relationships, daily interactions with people, and how they move through life. We see it from the White House to our house. Sometimes it's masked and other times everyone around can see it but the person dealing with it.

Some of us may have faced many types of trauma in the past, while others are currently going through a traumatic experience right now. Your trauma doesn't have to look like mine. It can look like anything from death of a loved one, church hurt, betrayal, sexual abuse, physical abuse, domestic violence, child abuse, divorce, or even serious injury. Trauma looks different for each of us depending on our own personal experiences.

I have listed some symptoms to recognize if you or someone you know has experienced trauma. I can honestly tell you that I've experienced many of these feelings as I fought mentally to deal with all three losses. You don't have to display all the symptoms for it to have a negative impact on your body. Take some time to jot down the ones you are experiencing.

Emotional Signs to Trauma

1. Denial
2. Anger
3. Sadness
4. Emotional outburst
5. Redirected emotions
6. A shattered sense of security
7. Anxiety
8. Unable to trust
9. Feeling disconnected
10. Struggling with upsetting memories and flashbacks
11. Depression
12. Substance Abuse
13. Always feeling unsafe
14. Avoiding anything that evokes memories of the traumatic event
15. Sadness
16. Rage
17. Constantly on guard
18. Insomnia
19. Avoiding crowds
20. Unable to discuss the experience
21. Suspicion of people
22. Self-blame
23. Loss of identity
24. Low self-esteem

25. Difficulty forming healthy adult relationships

Physical Signs of Trauma

1. Lethargy
2. Poor concentration
3. Panic attacks
4. Finding it hard to cope
5. Fatigue
6. Insomnia
7. Night terrors
8. Dreams
9. Agitation
10. Weight Loss
11. Negative health impacts (i.e. high blood pressure, heart disease and various autoimmune diseases, etc.)
12. Anger
13. Rage
14. Mood swings
15. Stress
16. Hair Loss
17. Appetite Loss
18. Memory Loss
19. Mental disorders

Spiritual Signs of Trauma

1. Lost trust in God
2. Feelings of being abandoned or punished by God
3. Unable to fully allow God to minister to you
4. Impaired outlook on spiritual matters
5. Changes in belief system
6. View anyone or anything associated with spiritual institutions as an enemy
7. Diminished participation in religious activities
8. Loss of meaning for living
9. Unable to understand life's purpose
10. Negative outlook on life
11. Lack of self-confidence
12. Impeded development
13. Depression and anxiety
14. Shame and guilt
15. Isolation
16. Difficulty creating boundaries

List any symptoms that you can identify below:

_____

_____

_____

Trauma can affect any of us at any time and is no respecter of persons. It can occur without notice or warning. It can be associated with things or events you were never prepared to face and can happen more than once in your life.

The sooner you recognize and address it, the better chances you have of not allowing these emotions to get out of control and have a negative impact on your body. The earlier you address trauma, the better chance you have of a full, successful recovery. Unaddressed trauma can have long-lasting effects that fester into something bigger if not handled. One of the best ways to treat trauma is seeking help to learn better ways to cope so you are equipped to handle the work that will need to be done during and after the experience.

Just because you block out the trauma doesn't mean it didn't happen and because you found what you believe are ways to cope doesn't mean that they are the right ways. You could be damaging yourself internally and never know how it's affecting your physical body. These things progressively build over time.

The human body doesn't want to willingly deal with trauma. We all find ways to suppress some of the negative experiences that happen in our lives by dressing up the pain or burying it like it never happened. It's easier to ignore how it made us feel. I did. To be honest, things were happening back to back so quickly that there was little time to grieve as I should or sulk in the pain. Keeping busy helped me keep my thoughts under control for the most part, or at least that's what I thought but the damage it caused internally was unseen. We can all walk around appearing okay on the surface, but it doesn't mean we are truly okay inside.

Below is a list of things that you can do to cope:

1. Seek counseling from a qualified professional
2. Prayer and meditation
3. Find a support group
4. Give yourself time to recognize you can't control everything that happens in your life
5. Journal your feelings
6. Don't make life changing decisions based on feelings of the present moment you're in
7. Get proper rest, nutrition, and exercise for the benefits of your mental health
8. Surround yourself with friends, family or do things you enjoy to avoid feeling withdrawn
9. Take moments to pull away and regroup when you feel stress, hurt or grief coming on
10. Make sure you have daily structure

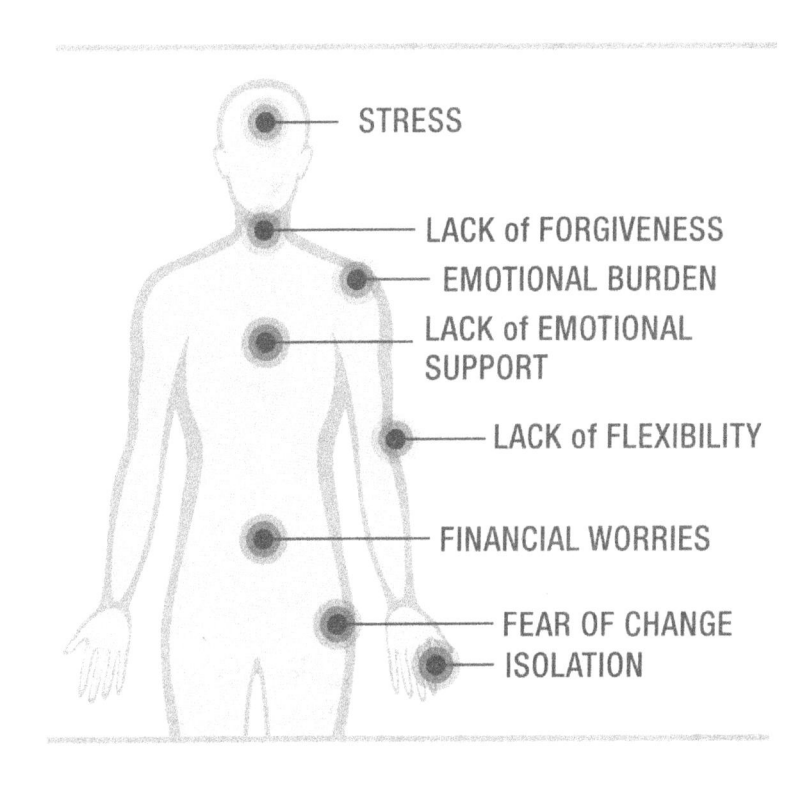

This diagram shows the physical effects of emotional trauma on your body.

ROUND SEVEN

Fighting Through Grief

*Blessed are those who mourn, for they
will be comforted.*
—Matthew 5:4 NIV

Constantly moving allowed me not to feel or deal with many emotions. While others may have grieved and found ways to cope and move on, I silently fought my battles and prayed to God. Yet my need for help never stood in the way of being able to encourage those around me who needed me. I continued to give you what I truly didn't have for myself. Even in the midst I was able to be the listening ear and give a word of encouragement to whomever needed it when I needed it myself. Still, I was grieving and struggling to cope with multiple tragic deaths.

Losing my grandma while going through things at home was a heavy burden to carry. Trying to grieve and continuing to handle day to day obligations and responsibilities was the hardest time of my life. Some days I did not know if I was coming or going. Each time I faced tragedy I never thought I could or would make it. I never even thought I had the strength or power to press but I did. Most days I did not even want to get out of bed, but God carried me. I woke up many mornings with tears already in my eyes from just an overwhelming pain.

My grandmother was someone I could never imagine being without. I could talk to her and tell her anything and by the end of the call I felt better. She was one of my confidants and I lost that part of me when she passed. Her death had lasting impacts that no one will ever understand. Losing her left a void that I never wanted to feel. I didn't think I could make it through a day not talking to her and even that was a process to get over. Many days her number rang in my head and I had the urge to pick up the phone to dial the number only to remind myself that she's no longer here.

I visited her grave still in shock that I would never see her on this side of heaven again. Flabbergasted, I just stood there in a cemetery surrounded by too many dead loved ones. I'd never hear those heartfelt messages she left on my phone again. Truthfully, I walked around most days after her death not okay but always found a way to keep functioning. I kept my appearance up with a made-up face. However, I never sought counseling to assist me in processing that tremendous loss. Countless hours were spent trying to find a message she may have left on my cell phone or house phone voicemail.

    Navigating loss of my beloved family caused me to live extremely guarded and in fear. I built a safety net in the back of my mind to be on the lookout for the next bad thing so I wouldn't be caught off guard again. Thus, it was hard for me to relish in any happy moments because I felt like I needed to protect myself so I wouldn't get knocked off my feet again. It was almost like I tried to prepare for the next loss I'd face no matter the capacity. It made me think I could just keep maneuvering my way through life bottling up so many hurt emotions and trauma as long as I was protected and ready for whatever was coming next. In the midst of the pain and grief, I continued being a lifeline for those connected to me. I was a natural encourager and a fighter when many did not know the fight it took for me to sail through every single day. Everyone was oblivious to what I was going through. They never knew the anguish that resided behind the smile they saw. This truth is all too familiar for many who had to bore the excruciating burden of grief.

The Stages of Grief after Trauma

1. **Denial** – *"This can't be happening."*

I experienced denial when I received the calls that my brother had been stabbed and the other killed by SWAT. My brain wouldn't allow me to accept that I was experiencing these traumas.

2. **Anger** – *"Why did this happen?"*

When my grandmother passed there were moments I was pissed at the hospital and all involved in her care. *How could a simple procedure be deadly for her?*

3. **Bargaining** – *"Make this go away and I'll do this or that." God, please just make this go away."*

When my brother faced time for the death of our brother, I knew I had to step in. I felt like it was the only thing to do. Crying out to God if He could just spare his life and praying for the judge and all who had the power to make decisions who affected the outcome. I was willing to sacrifice my time, money, tears and effort if God would just honor my request.

4. **Depression** – *"I feel so sad." "I just don't want to do anything that I used to do."*

I felt lost after the deaths and most days like I was floating on air. I wasn't sure how to be or what to do. I felt guilty for living and as if I did not have a right for the moments I would laugh or smile. I wondered how I could be smiling when my loved one just died.

5. **Acceptance** – *"This is hard, but I have to move forward."*

As hard as it was, I eventually had to get to the point where it was necessary for me to become brave enough to take the steps to heal. I had to finally accept that they were no longer here with me. I had to find ways to focus on the good memories and not constantly rehearse how they died. I also had to realize that all of these emotions were normal, and I had the right to feel each of them.

ROUND EIGHT

Fighting for Healing

*Courage doesn't happen when you have
all the answers. It happens when you are
ready to face the questions you've been
avoiding your whole life.*
—Shannon L. Alder

Whether told or untold we all have a story and a reason we behave the way we do but most times there isn't anyone to dig deep enough to find out why. Jails are filled with a lot of untold stories, hurts and pain. The cells are lined with traumas and realities that may have been experienced and never addressed until it took a turn for the negative outcome. People are walking around just "handling it." They are coping the best way they know how and managing like I did, like my family did until the next tragic event in life happens.

Everyone deals with trauma differently but one thing I would suggest is that you make it a priority to seek help and talk through it. It doesn't matter if it's the loss of a loved one, hurt or a traumatic experience. Each one has a way of negatively affecting our lives if we don't allow ourselves the time needed to deal with it or go through the necessary stages that happen with each one.

Going through all the experiences shared I never sought help outside for any of the deaths. I had my moments of crying and dealing with the numerous triggers that came up and I handled them in my own way and moved on until the next one came--and there is *always* a next one. I never discussed it with people around me. As horrible as the losses were, our family grieved the best way we knew how and continued with life. Managing. Managing pains, memories and emotions that were so unbearable to the human mind and body that we were not equipped to handle, much less address, on our own.

We can sometimes feel ashamed to seek counseling. In certain communities it's shunned, causing us to refuse help. As an African American, you never really heard much talk of going to seek a therapist, especially around the time I went through multiple losses. Even now, we're just starting to realize that it's okay not to be okay and seek help. Some of us in the Black community grew up believing that we never ever aired our dirty laundry outside the house. What goes on in the house stays in the house couldn't be further from the truth. That very mentality has become a detriment to our communities today. We have a lot of people walking around mentally ill, suffering in silence, having identity crises, passing their dysfunction on to generation after generation and acting out in different ways that have destroyed us if we really look deep enough. I don't care what the circumstances are, if you look deep enough it all goes back to something we may have dealt with personally or witnessed. Sometimes the way we address things or not stems from our environments and how we saw it. Not always, but most of the time.

Even with all of that, many of us still don't see the value but desperately need to reach out to a professional therapist to work through some of the deep pain. It took me years to sit here and have the courage to begin writing about what I went through. Only those close to me will know of the numerous tragedies but it's never been something I've openly discussed in public with most.

I spent years burying hurt after hurt and it did more harm than good by not addressing it. I didn't allow myself the time I needed to feel to just be and let it out no matter how it made me or anyone around me feel. Never releasing the emotions that were ripping me apart inside caused me so much turmoil, but I had to be the strong one. That cycle created layers of pain that got pushed down until the next thing happened and the next thing. I made myself look good on the outside in attempts to feel good inside, but I was terribly broken internally. I went out of my way helping those around me in hopes of it helping me. Suffering in silence and not giving anyone a clue as to the extent of what I was feeling. No one could ever understand anyway, and it only made me mad when people said they did. *How can you understand if you never walked a day in my shoes?*

There's no way you can imagine the magnitude of what our family endured or feel the pain if you personally never felt it, but we handled it the best way we could. We gave the appearance that we were okay, when in fact we were not okay which leads me to my next concern. How many of you have experienced a traumatic event in your life and just buried the events and pain? Did you ever seek help? Probably not as many who should have. Do you think that having read my experiences that I could have handled it alone without counseling? The answer is *no*, but back then it wasn't a priority. I've always been an introverted, quiet and reserved person but these experiences caused me to crawl into my shell even more. No, I didn't want to go talk to a counselor. I thought I was okay. Like so many others, I just did not see the value in therapy.

Growing up, I saw the women in my family just fight to keep going no matter. You did what you had to. Women were the ones to hold the families down. Just push through no matter what was going on in our lives. The back bones of the family. There was an appearance to uphold. You fought feelings silently or between another sister who may have been fighting her own secret battles, personal hurts, losses, and trauma. There were things that her and only God knew about. She knew that no matter what was happening behind closed doors or within families that once she was in public, she had to keep it together. As women, we continued to maneuver through generational dysfunction, hurt, trauma, loss and pain.

Suppression of feelings is a normal thing for some, and the cycle just continues. Keep busy. Take care of home, family and whatever else we must face with life's daily responsibilities. We hardly ever, if at all, stop to do a self-check to see if we are okay. We are everything for everyone else. We encourage everyone else until we have nothing left to give and hardly ever receive that same level of care when we need it. I saw it all too often in my family and grew up watching it. All the dysfunctions that shape our realities and shape how we move through life and deal with things that come our way. In many cases, it is how we learn to process and handle life.

In most of the Black communities growing up, if boys/men cried or shared anything that resembled emotions or tears they were labeled weak. People looked at them funny. Boys don't cry. I heard all too often that big boys don't cry. Be a man. Crying is for babies and all the other crazy things we said that caused people to feel that they couldn't express pain. Those words have some men today walking around with so much built up hurt and anger and no skills for coping with the negative things that affect their lives. They are unable to cry, hug and display affection all for the sake of being "strong." That's a dangerous space to be in.

My brothers found themselves in one of those dangerous situations and may have been going through something internally. The emotions that were deep inside of Brandon kept him from going to counseling thinking he could handle it alone or that he didn't need professional help to work through his feelings. He was ashamed to let his guard down for fear of the sound or appearance of going to a therapist.

Like many, I too had a misconception of therapy and felt it was weird to go sit and tell this total stranger all my innermost feelings. The thought of pouring my guts out to someone who would only judge me was not a great idea to me. It's probably the same way my brother felt. In his mind, he may have felt that he really was being strong until it started to slowly affect him mentally. For me it seemed easier because I had a family to take care of, a business and people who needed and depended on me. I was the go-to person and the one people always found easy to talk to, when I actually needed to talk and deal with all the bottled-up feelings I had.

I'm not aware that my mom or any of my siblings sought help for the losses we faced either. It was just something we didn't do. Why is counseling something we avoid in the Black community? Why is there a negative stigma attached to going to counseling outside the church?

On more than one occasion, I tried getting my brother to seek counseling because I could see what was happening with him. The outward changes in him and when I learned that he had sought help and was given meds that he wasn't taking them saddened me. Could it be that my brother's coping mechanisms were to bury those feelings and act strong when in fact he wasn't? Could he have possibly thought that it was a sign of weakness to seek help and the idea of taking medicine was something he just couldn't bring himself to do because he didn't want to be labeled as crazy. I wasn't around him every day and had no idea what his day to day life was like or what else he could have been dealing with. He always declined the idea of counseling and would always say I'm okay just like how young boys were taught in some of our communities. You fall, pick yourself up and keep moving. That's what he did but sadly it wasn't okay. He left this world dealing with mental illness, but he did not have to deal with it alone. He could have sought help.

The truth is that there may come a time when we all may need to seek help and it's perfectly okay. It doesn't make us crazy. It's time we dispel the myth that seeking help from a therapist is considered weak and only for white people. It's also time that we reprogram our minds against the attitudes we grew up with about seeking help. You can't do it alone. Trust me. I couldn't and it took years to come to this reality and I want you to see it for yourself too.

Don't spend years going through the agonizing pain I went through thinking that I had it together but was nowhere even close. Years later and I just now began to open up about the deaths that if not for God's grace would have knocked me off my feet. These unwanted realities were enough to have me in the same mindset as my brother, but God's grace kept me. No, I didn't handle it well or maneuver through it the right way, but I am still here to share my story with you.

It took a while to find a therapist just right for me, but I did. It took joining a ministry that taught deep healing and deliverance for it all to come together, along with lots of self-development and for me to see that I am not what I went through. I am not what happened to me and my story matters. No matter how hurtful it is, there is a reason God took me through it and my pain plays a big part in me fulfilling my purpose.

I urge you to throw away the negative mindsets toward seeking a therapist and take the time to find the right fit for you. And surprise, your counselor may not be found in church and that's okay. So, don't look for your counselor in one place. I know that many of us were taught to take all our problems to the church, but the reality is that the church is full of people with their own stories, problems, wounds and trauma. You just may be surprised that you'll find a therapist outside the four walls of the church. Don't get me wrong there may be well-abled therapists there but don't dismiss outside therapy if that's where you find the person you can connect with. It wasn't until I found someone who I connected with that I was comfortable enough opening up.

For some, the thought disdain for counseling is due to the lack of cultural identities, experiences, and relationship values. People may feel counselors don't recognize or can't relate to many of the things that we are faced with in the African American community. They feel that therapists won't be able to relate if they're white. There is a chance that they may even be labeled and misdiagnosed and due to racial disparities, there is also a lack of trust. Some don't go because there is a shortage of people who look like them. Go to any counseling facility or look at any roster. You will find that there is a very small percentage of African American counselors.

Honestly, I've felt like that before. Some of the times that I went to counseling I felt judged because the woman just sat there the whole time and listened to me pour my guts out not saying a word only to end with, "Okay, what time next week?" I left feeling deflated, thinking this Caucasian woman can never really understand the struggles I have faced.

Then there were other times I sensed that they just weren't the right fit for me. No real connection. To be transparent, you may have to go through a few to find the right fit for you but don't get discouraged. You're worth taking the time to pray and seek the right person for you and your needs. Sometimes that person may not be in your local church assembly or the therapist that worked for your friend and that's okay. You'll find the right fit. As with anything, sometimes we must go through a few bad apples to get the best one and I'm grateful I did.

    I recognize now that I really needed and should have sought help much earlier. Then, of course, there are thoughts that I should have been more forceful about my brother getting help. Going to counseling doesn't make you crazy. In fact, it makes you someone who has the courage to face your fears and come out stronger than you ever thought you could. It puts you on the path to becoming an overcomer and using your life experiences to help shape you into a much stronger person.

    It doesn't mean that the trauma didn't happen, but counseling will put you on the path to becoming whole again. It will enable you to peel back the layers of unresolved pain, allowing you to process what happened to you in a healthier way. It takes strength to face our fears, hurts and deeply rooted pain. For years I fought it and it did more harm than good. These stories I've shared with you are just the beginning of finally releasing some of my experiences.

    As I type this, I am reminded that I never thought I'd see this day, but here I am praying that you feel my heart and take my recommendation. If you found yourself relating to anything that I shared, acknowledge that it may be an area that needs attention. You know those signs I had you jot down? If any still trigger you, then maybe it's time you address it once and for all. You may not need ongoing therapy but just take the first step and make the call today. I promise you'll feel better. I do and I'm continuing to work on getting better. It takes time and won't happen overnight, but it can happen.

ROUND NINE

Fighting for Destiny

"For I know the plans I have for you," declares the Lord, "plans to prosper you and not to harm you, plans to give you hope and a future.
—*Jeremiah 29:11 NIV*

I seriously struggled starting to write this book. So many times, I would start only to get to those pieces of me that still feel hurt when I talk or write about it. Yet here I am finally being brave enough to open up. Honestly, I can't count how many times I've been in church and been prophesied to write the books by total strangers. Just the thought of opening up about areas of my life that I could never fully share with people around me because most wouldn't understand was so daunting. But here I am starting to peel back those pieces that crushed my heart in hopes that it helps to heal yours.

Some may ask why. I did it for you because I know many of you are either going through trauma now or have experienced your own trauma. That's why you were drawn to this book. If one person reading this book becomes healed then this was worth the late nights, the anxiety and palpitations while writing, the restless nights, the open wounds I felt sometimes as I was writing, the heaviness in my chest, the wishing my brothers were still here and wondering what they would have become, the wishing I could make life a bit easier for my brother who served time, and the wishing my mom hadn't loss her children to violent deaths. If the only person who becomes healed is you, then it was well worth it.

I got up the courage to reach back and share my experiences in hopes that you know you're not alone. I pray that you know I too have felt like I couldn't make it and wanted to give up. The feelings of being alone and misunderstood have overtaken me. I've suppressed the feelings and allowed people to rush my healing with comments like, 'you should be over it,' not fully understanding the pain I was in. I was suffering silently like maybe some of you are.

The truth is you can't get over anything if you don't process the feelings of trauma. No one has the right to rush your process along no matter what the circumstances are. You must go through and feel every single emotion, the good, the bad and the ugly. No one can put a limit on the process and until you deal with the pain it will continue to be there. They say time heals all pain. Yes, that may be true, but what are you doing during that time? It's taken me years to get here and I'm still uncovering and processing. There's still many more books to come full of layers to the healing process.

    I'm here now just writing this book because I believe God wants to use me to heal and as proof that it doesn't happen overnight. It's a process but how long or short the process is dependent on us. God has a purpose for my pain. As I type years later, I know that there is so much more to me and so much healing that still needs to happen, but I've taken another step in my journey. Writing this book is a step in the right direction. What I don't want is for you to go through years like I have and not deal with what's hurting you. It's time to address what keeps you up at night and the triggers that you bury for fear of finally having to deal with it. I've gone through so much that I felt like God forgot about me and my sacrifices to fight for others. Sometimes I wonder if He bottled up the tears that I cried silently at night. I know what it feels like to fight those battles and wish you could pour your heart out and just maybe it would feel better. I am all too familiar with feeling all alone even when you're surrounded by many people.

Often, I was reminded of the poem, "Footprints in the Sand." The poem reflects upon a dream of walking along the beach with the Lord. Scenes of my life have flashed in mind where I could see two sets of prints. Then there are those heart-wrenching moments when I lost my brothers that I look back on and noticed only one set of footprints. I noticed that at what seemed to be the lowest and saddest times in life it felt like one print disappeared. The one print left was all that I needed to carry me through. That's all we need. The Lord.

I felt like sometimes I was alone and no one else understood just how much pain I was in. No one understood how sad I was. *What is the reason this all happened? Why did my loved ones have to endure pain dying how they did?* As I sat and reflected on the poem, for once I just wanted the Lord to allow me to ask Him these things. As I continued to walk through these tragic steps, the poem reminded me that God loves me and would never leave me. He would never leave me through trials and tests. He reminded me that He would never leave me alone through some of the worst periods of my life.

God reminded me through this poem that all those times I felt this way He was indeed right beside me. The times I physically walked alone that He was always carrying me, giving me the strength that I needed to push through, to fight and be the light in dark situations. He was there when I didn't have the right words to pray and nothing would come out. Those are the times that He carried me, and God is carrying you too. Allow Him to. I paraphrased a lot of the poem, but I would invite you to go read it as it's written and keep it with you so that when those times come you are reminded that you are not alone.

    I came for you after all these years because you needed to hear from someone who could relate to you and not the statements people often make who may have never felt what we have or share the same experiences. They mean well but hearing from someone who truly does know will touch the parts of you that many have not been able to relate to. If I'm able to touch your life and you get a breakthrough and you finally seek help to deal with the wounds that you haven't been able to heal then guess what? This book was worth the blood, sweat and tears it cost me!

    As painful as it was to go through this, I know it too serves a purpose. It's my truth. It's part of my story and it's evidence and a track record of a loving God who kept me and I couldn't have gone through this and not share my experience no matter how long it took to write the book.

We may not understand it at the time but everything in our life serves a purpose good or bad. I came back for you because you too are a part of my story because God knew the ones who needed to hear from me. He knew you would pick up this book. He knows that you too have inner wounds that need healing that may go way back that you haven't addressed. God knows the part of this book that hits those spots that you still may be avoiding.

How do I know? Because it's what I did also. I truly know how frustrating it can become when starting to heal. You want to fight it as long as possible to avoid feeling the feelings and the truth is no matter how it looks like you're on top of things on the outside the only person you're really fooling is you. Allow yourself the time to go through and be human. Don't allow the people around you to make you skip the necessary steps in the healing process. Your feelings are valid, and they matter. Every single one of them. Whether they believe they do or not.

It's okay not to be okay. Say it out loud now. No, really. Say it aloud. *It's okay not to be okay.* I wished someone had told me that as I was going through. I walked around like I was on my A-game most times still encouraging from a broken place. I said the words to women I wished someone would have said to me. I ministered to women when I was secretly ministering to myself. I encouraged others from brokenness, from hurt, pain and grief. Grieving is a hard thing for anyone to go through but it's even harder when it's traumatic experiences like the ones I went through.

I don't know your story, nor do I know the grief, the pain, or what category your trauma falls under. What I do know is that God loves you and you're here to read this book which means that His hands are still on you too and He wants to heal you. He wants to minister to those secret spots that you hide and run from. You know the ones you hear people talking about that trigger that pain point that you want to act as if it never happened to you. Yup, those ones. Those secret spots that make you relive the trauma all over again. That hidden spot that creates the ache in your heart like the heaviness I felt as I typed this book. You see it's easy to ignore it but hard as hell to relive, break down and fight to move past your trauma.

One thing I always made sure of was that I looked good on the outside, but the truth is I was a sad and broken vessel inside fighting to become all that God had created me to be because I spent years carrying pain and being strong for everyone else. Years of my life were dedicated to worrying about everyone else and skipping processes because I didn't want to deal with hurt. Pain is uncomfortable and it's going to take all you have to process through it. You see just how long it's taken me, but I don't want that for you. You can decide now. Nothing I went through killed me. No matter how utterly painful it was I am still here to share my story.

As I end this book, I don't want you to close it without finally opening up and making a promise to yourself that you will finally deal with those areas my experiences touched. You owe it to yourself to become free. Free to release the pain and move forward in life knowing that if you're still here to read this book your life has meaning and purpose. It's time to heal.

    I came for you. I endured to share my pain with you to provoke you to run after your healing. You can decide to dump the weight that's been holding you back. Please don't let this be just another book. Don't ignore those pain points you felt. Don't ignore the triggers any longer.

    I came for you. I believe you were drawn to this book for a reason. My heart was dumped out into this book so that you would become free. Healing can be yours here and now if you would just make up your mind today before closing this book that you're going to start the process. Decide that today is the first day of the last day allowing yourself to hold you back because of your story. Our stories are different, but our outcomes can be the same. Get free, heal and get ready for God to use you and your story.

I came for you. Now you heal and break free so you can reach back and free someone else. That is my prayer with this book. Someone is waiting on you just like you were waiting on me to write this book. I came for you now who will you come for? God wants to deliver and heal you from your own trauma. Someone is waiting on you. The longer we keep our stories inside, the longer someone else is delayed in their healing. Will you take the steps to answer the call? It all starts and ends with you. True healing and freedom can be yours today. Take the necessary steps to move forward. It doesn't have to take you years like it did for me. I want that for you, but do you want it for yourself? It's time. I may not know you, but I love you. I know this book may not be for everyone, but it is for the ones who can relate to the places I'm coming from.

Be Healed.

ACKNOWLEDGMENTS

I would like to express my sincere thanks and appreciation for the love and support I received from my husband and children during these very trying times. Matthew, you carried the weight of financially making sure my brothers had everything they needed as they were laid to rest. You stood by my side and held me when you didn't know the words to say to help me through these traumas.

To my three hearts, my children Kayode, Adekemi and Kameron: You were my reasons to push when life wanted me to give up. When I felt I couldn't make it, your beautiful faces allowed me to keep fighting day by day knowing brighter days were ahead. I had to fight for you. You will always and forever be my why.

To Charmaine Shaffer-Terrell, I don't know what I would have done without you. Thank you for always sitting with my kids as I fought for my brother. You selflessly cared for my infant son while I was away at court.

Mom, thank you for the sacrifices and encouraging words.

To my remaining siblings, I love you for you who are in my life. Each of us with different and unique bonds.

Lachelle McNeal Thorbs, I love you girl! You have always been by my side and not only supported but encouraged me. We may not see each other much but I know and can always trust that you had my back.

Lastly, to the three pieces of our family tree that were broken here on earth. My dear grandmother, whom I love deeply and hold so close to my heart every day. You helped to shape me into the woman I am today, and I am forever grateful for the unbreakable bond that we shared. You are and will forever live in my heart. To my brothers Brandon and Lorenzo, I miss you guys so much. When I saw one, I saw the other and to not see either of you is hard. Pieces of our family tree were broken here on earth when the three of you left, but you will forever remain in my heart.

ABOUT THE AUTHOR

Tasha Odunuyi is one of the voices of our generation who God is using to empower women to lived healed and free. Armed with courage, she shares the trauma and pain that she has experienced for the sole purpose of helping others.

In addition to her passion of seeing others set free, she is also the owner of Diella Designs where she channels her creative energy into designing custom statement pieces. With the belief that we are destined to have multiple streams of income, Tasha is also a licensed real estate broker and home stager. Everything that she does helps to position women to live their best lives, whether it's through their attire or by helping them to become homeowners.

Tasha's greatest prize is her family. Residing in the northwest suburbs of Chicago, she shares her life with her loving husband and three beautiful children.

Find out more about Tasha's company at dielladesigns.com.